MARCUS WAREING

WITH JENI WRIGHT

HOW TO COOK
THE PERFECT...

LONDON NEW YORK MUNICH MELBOURNE DELHI

For my family – Jane, Jake, Archie and Jessie – with love, Marcus

Project Editor Norma MacMillan
Project Art Editors and Designers Smith & Gilmour London
Photographer David Loftus
Cover photographer Georgia Glynn Smith

Senior Editor Dawn Henderson
Senior Art Editor Susan Downing
Cover Design & Art Direction Nicola Powling
DTP Designer Traci Salter
Production Controller Luca Frassinetti

First published in Great Britain in 2007, by Dorling Kindersley Limited
80 Strand, London WC2R 0RL

This edition published in 2014

Penguin Group (UK)

Copyright © 2007, 2014 Dorling Kindersley
Text copyright © 2007, 2014 Marcus Wareing
Photographs copyright © 2007, 2014 Dorling Kindersley

2 4 6 8 10 9 7 5 3 1

A CIP catalogue record for this book is available from the British Library

ISBN: 978 0 2411 8784 5

Colour reproduction by MDP, UK
Printed by Canale in Romania

Discover more at
www.dk.com

Author's note: I always cook in a fan-assisted oven, both at home and in the restaurant, and all of the recipes in this book have been tested in a domestic fan-assisted oven. I've given the temperatures for cooking in a conventional oven, both electric and gas, too. If you're using a conventional oven, double check these equivalents in your manufacturer's handbook.

CONTENTS

MY CHARTER FOR SUCCESSFUL COOKING

All the years I've been cooking it's struck me how much more there is to know in a recipe than what's written down. There's a level of understanding that professionals have that most readers don't, and very few recipe books provide it. This led me to thinking how good it would be to dig really deep into my recipes and strip them back to the basics, pinpointing the whys and wherefores and even the pitfalls, and sharing the key to perfection for each and every one. So this is what I've done in this book, and I'm sure it will give you the confidence to tackle any dish you like, even if you've never cooked it before. But before you start, please read my 10-point charter for success. In my restaurants and at home I always follow these same, simple rules. If you follow them too, I guarantee you'll not only enjoy cooking, but you'll get perfect results every time.

1
Plan ahead before you start cooking
Read the recipe from start to finish, making sure you understand both the ingredients and the method. If you can do this the day before, so much the better.

2
Keep a good storecupboard
Staple items in your cupboard and fridge will provide the basis for good meals, and save you time.

3
Make a shopping list
Check what you've got, and write down what you haven't.

4
Shop for fresh ingredients on the day
Buy only as much as you need, and take time to source the best.

5
Read the recipe again
Sit down, take your time, and make a plan of action, allowing adequate time for each step.

6
Dress the part
Put your apron on and clear your working area, then set out your stall by assembling all the ingredients and equipment.

7
Be prepared
Before starting to cook, weigh and measure ingredients and complete any preparation steps like peeling, slicing, and chopping.

8
Tidy and clean as you go
Keep your workstation clear of clutter at all times, from starting the recipe to serving the dish.

9
Re-organize
If things aren't going to plan, stop, take stock, and re-organize, then carry on.

10
Enjoy cooking
Last but not least, relax and be confident. The food will taste better for it.

SOUPS

CHINESE NOODLE SOUP

When I'm in a big city, wherever it is in the world, I always go to Chinatown. Seeing Chinese people there eating noodle soup tells me it must be good, and I just love the powerful flavour of the broth with the simple vegetables and noodles. When I recreate noodle soup at home and want to make it into a more substantial meal, I add strips of cooked chicken, duck, or beef at the end.

SERVES 4

1.5 litres Beef Stock (opposite)
4 celery sticks, strings removed and very finely sliced
1 carrot, peeled and pared into ribbons with a vegetable peeler, then cut into julienne
1 leek (white part only), very finely sliced
6 spring onions, very finely sliced
100g dried Chinese egg noodles (medium size)
Sea salt and freshly milled black pepper

TO SERVE
Soy sauce
Toasted sesame oil

Bring the stock to the boil over a high heat, then simmer for 15–20 minutes until reduced to about half its original volume. As the volume decreases, the flavour increases.

While the stock is simmering, bring a pan of salted water to the boil over a high heat. Add the vegetables, bring back to the boil, and blanch for 2 minutes. Lift out with a slotted spoon, transfer to a colander, and rinse under the cold tap.

Plunge the noodles into the vegetable blanching water and bring back to the boil, stirring to separate the strands. Simmer for 4 minutes, then drain.

Divide the vegetables and noodles among warmed bowls. Check and correct the seasoning of the stock, then ladle into the bowls on top of the vegetables and noodles. Serve straightaway, with soy sauce and sesame oil for seasoning at the table.

BEEF STOCK

MAKES ABOUT 1.5 LITRES
About 3kg beef bones, chopped
(ask your butcher to do this)
Vegetable oil, for frying
3 carrots, peeled and halved
crossways
2 onions, quartered lengthways
3 whole leeks, cut crossways
into 3cm lengths
½ bulb garlic (cut crossways)
3 celery sticks, halved crossways
3 sprigs of fresh or dried thyme
1 bay leaf
3tbsp tomato purée

Heat the oven to 200°C fan (220°C/gas 7). Roast the bones in a very large, heavy roasting pan for about 30 minutes until dark golden brown, turning them every 10 minutes or so. Lift the bones out and let the excess fat drain off, then put them in a very large, heavy pan. Pour in enough cold water to cover (about 4.5 litres) and bring to the boil.

Meanwhile, heat 4tbsp oil in a large, heavy pan and fry the carrots over a high heat until dark golden brown all over. Remove with a slotted spoon and drain in a colander. Repeat with the onions, then the leeks and garlic, and finally the celery, adding more oil as needed. Return all the vegetables to the pan and stir in the thyme, bay leaf, and tomato purée. Cook for about 5 minutes, and drain in a colander.

When the water reaches boiling point, skim, then add the vegetables. Bring back to the boil and skim again, then turn the heat down to very low. Cook very gently for 4–6 hours, uncovered, skimming regularly.

Ladle into a colander set over a bowl, then pass the strained stock through a muslin-lined sieve into a clean pan. Boil until reduced to about 1.5 litres. Use straightaway, or cool quickly and refrigerate in a covered container, then remove any surface fat before using.

KEY TO PERFECTION

Simple soups like this one rely on their stock for flavour and body, so you must get the stock right.

After roasting the bones, put them in a large sieve or colander set over a pan or bowl, and leave next to the stove for 10 minutes. This will drain off the fat, so you will have less skimming to do later and the stock will not be greasy.

During the long cooking time, keep the heat very low so the stock barely murmurs. Don't let the stock boil or fat will come out of the bones into the stock, and the vegetables will break down and make the stock cloudy.

Fat and scum make stock greasy and cloudy, so frequent skimming during simmering is essential. Use a ladle, taking care to keep it only just below the surface of the liquid.

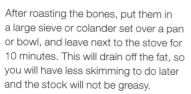

"For a fabulous dinner party main course, serve each portion topped with a steamed fillet of cod or sea bass."

FRENCH ONION SOUP

An absolute classic, this is one of the first soups I learnt to make at college, and it's also one of the first things I made when I was training at The Savoy hotel in London at the age of eighteen. I loved French onion soup then, and I love it just as much now.

SERVES 4
5 white-skinned onions, peeled
3tbsp vegetable oil
50g unsalted butter, diced
2 good sprigs of fresh thyme
5 garlic cloves, finely chopped
500ml red wine, either Burgundy or Bordeaux
1 litre hot Beef Stock (page 11)
Sea salt and freshly milled black pepper

TO FINISH
About 2tbsp finely chopped fresh chervil or parsley
Cheese Croûtes (below)

Halve the onions lengthways, place cut side down, and cut across into 5mm-thick slices. In a large, heavy pan, heat the oil and butter until foaming. Add the onions, thyme, and seasoning, and cook over a low to medium heat for a few minutes before stirring in the garlic. Cover and cook gently for 15–20 minutes, stirring frequently.

Pour in the wine, increase the heat to high, and boil rapidly for about 10 minutes until the wine has all but disappeared. Pour in the stock and bring to the boil, then skim off any fat or scum with a ladle. Simmer gently, uncovered, for 45 minutes to 1 hour, skimming occasionally.

To finish, check and correct the seasoning of the soup, then ladle into warmed bowls, packing them with plenty of onions. Sprinkle with chervil and top with the croûtes.

CHEESE CROÛTES

MAKES 16
16 thin slices of baguette
Olive oil, for drizzling
100g Gruyère or Cheddar cheese, grated

Heat the oven to 200°C fan (220°C/gas 7). Put the baguette slices on an oiled baking tray and drizzle with olive oil. Bake for 3–5 minutes until they are crisp and golden.

Turn the slices over and bake for another 3–5 minutes. Top with the grated cheese. Return to the oven (or pop under the grill) and bake for 1–2 minutes until melted.

"I always use small, compact onions with white skins for this soup. They have more flavour than large brown-skinned ones, which can be watery."

KEY TO PERFECTION

You need to get the consistency and colour of the onions right before adding the stock. At first they must be cooked until soft, but they must not be browned or the soup will taste bitter. Then they need to be saturated with wine to give the soup colour, body, and flavour.

At the end of boiling with the wine, the softened onions will become a deep burgundy red and almost dry. When you hear them start to sizzle on the bottom of the pan, it's time to take them off the heat.

Fry the onions gently at the beginning so they soften with only a very light colouring. Covering the pan helps, as the water from inside the lid drips onto them and keeps them moist.

PUMPKIN SOUP

Gordon Ramsay taught me this soup when we were working together at Aubergine in the early 90s. I've been making it ever since. When pumpkin isn't in season, it works just as well with butternut squash.

SERVES 6
1.4kg ripe pumpkin
100g unsalted butter
1.3 litres hot Chicken Stock (below)
100g fresh Parmesan cheese, grated
3–4tbsp double cream
Sea salt and freshly milled black pepper

TO SERVE
Extra-virgin olive oil
Shavings of fresh Parmesan cheese

Cut the pumpkin into chunks and scrape out the seeds, then peel off the tough skin. Slice the pumpkin flesh thinly.

Heat the butter in a large, heavy saucepan over a medium-high heat until it foams and turns nut brown. Add the pumpkin, sprinkle with salt, and stir well, then turn the heat down to low. Cover and cook gently for 15 minutes, shaking the pan from time to time.

Pour in the hot stock, increase the heat to high, and bring to the boil. Add the Parmesan and stir in, then turn the heat down to a gentle simmer. Cook uncovered for 15 minutes, stirring occasionally so the Parmesan doesn't stick on the bottom of the pan.

Purée the soup in a blender, working in batches, then pass the purée through a fine sieve into a clean pan. Whisk in the cream. Reheat the soup gently, then taste and correct the seasoning if necessary.

Ladle the soup into warmed bowls, drizzle over some olive oil, and top with Parmesan shavings. Serve straightaway.

CHICKEN STOCK

MAKES ABOUT 1.3 LITRES
1 organic chicken weighing about 1.5kg
2 onions, cut into 2cm pieces
1 leek (both green and white parts), cut into 2cm pieces
3 celery sticks, cut into 2cm pieces
1/2 bulb garlic (cut crossways)
1 sprig of fresh or dried thyme
2 bay leaves
Sea salt

Remove the breasts from the chicken and use for another dish. Chop the rest of the chicken in half and wash in cold water, then put in a large, heavy saucepan and cover with cold water. Bring to the boil over a high heat and skim off the scum with a ladle.

When the stock is clear of scum, add the vegetables, garlic, thyme, and bay leaves, and bring back to the boil. Skim again, turn the heat down to a very gentle simmer, and cook uncovered for 2½ hours, skimming regularly. Towards the end of cooking, taste and add salt. You should add the salt a little at a time until you get the correct seasoning.

Strain the stock through a fine sieve into a clean pan or bowl, pressing down on the bones and vegetables with a ladle to get all the liquid from them. Use the stock straightaway, or cool quickly and refrigerate in a covered container, then remove any surface fat before using.

KEY TO PERFECTION

For a velvety texture, the pumpkin must be thoroughly cooked at each stage or it won't purée smoothly in the blender.

Put the lid on the saucepan while the pumpkin is cooking in the butter at the beginning. This will make the pumpkin sweat so that moisture will drip from inside the lid into the pan.

When the pumpkin has had a full 15 minutes gently sweating in butter, it will break up and release its juices. This is the cue for adding the stock.

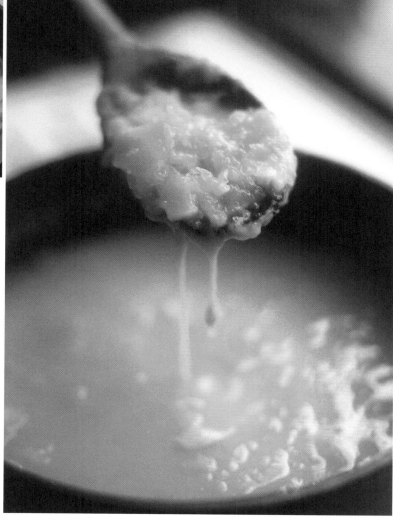

At the end of simmering in the stock, you will know the pumpkin is ready for blending when it's as soft as butter.

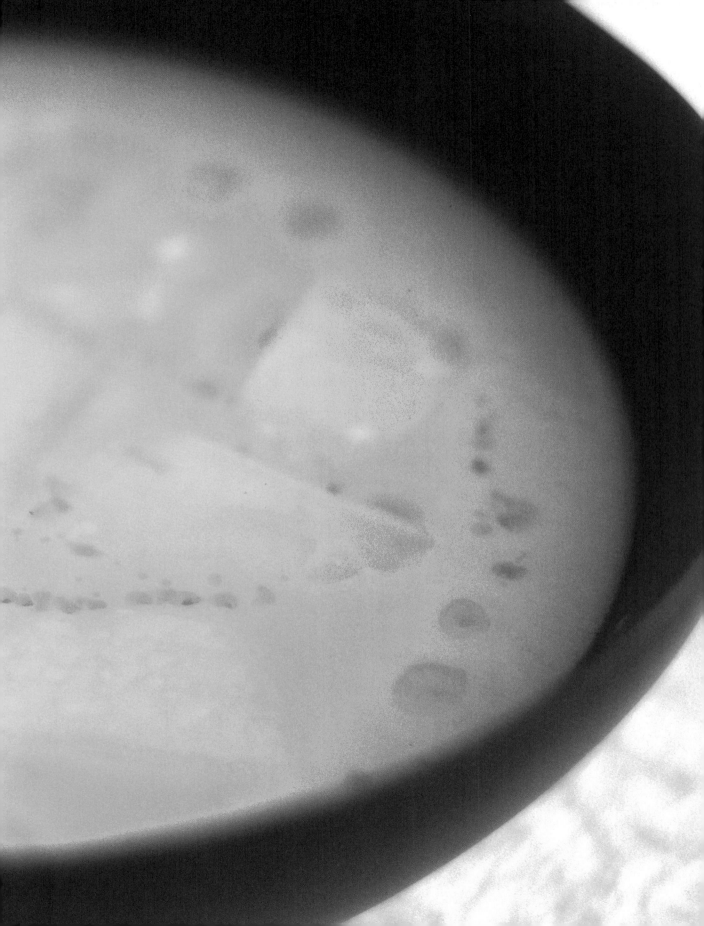

MUSHROOM SOUP

The intense mushroom flavour of this soup is its *raison d'être*, and I don't try to camouflage it. The cream and butter make it very rich and silky smooth, and they don't detract from the flavour at all.

SERVES 4–6
750g wide cap field mushrooms
125ml olive oil
3 large shallots, finely sliced
2 garlic cloves, finely chopped
Juice of 1/2 lemon
1 litre hot Chicken Stock (page 16)
250ml double cream
100g unsalted butter, diced
Sea salt and freshly milled
white pepper

**FOR THE SHALLOT
AND HERB CREAM**
5tbsp double cream
1–2 small shallots, finely diced
1 sprig each of fresh chervil,
tarragon, and coriander,
finely chopped
A few stems of fresh chives,
finely snipped

Wipe the mushrooms clean with a damp cloth, then slice them thinly. Heat the oil in a large, heavy pan. Add the shallots and cook over a low heat for a few minutes until softened, then stir in the garlic and soften for a minute or two longer. Add the mushrooms and sprinkle with a little salt. Increase the heat to get the mushrooms cooking, then toss and stir to mix them with the shallots and garlic. Cover and cook gently for 5–8 minutes, stirring occasionally.

Squeeze in the lemon juice and reduce a little, then pour in the stock and stir well. Increase the heat to high and bring to the boil. Turn the heat down and simmer uncovered for 10 minutes, stirring occasionally, until the mushrooms are really soft.

Purée the soup in a blender in batches, adding the cream while the machine is running. Keep blending until smooth.

Make the shallot and herb cream by lightly whipping the cream, then adding the shallots, herbs, and seasoning. Fold the ingredients together until well combined.

To finish, pour the soup into a clean pan and heat through, whisking in the diced butter until melted. Taste for seasoning, then ladle into warmed bowls and top with the shallot and herb cream.

"Only use field mushrooms for this soup, and don't worry if they're past their prime and starting to shrivel. Older mushrooms contain less water than very fresh mushrooms, so their flavour is more concentrated."

KEY TO PERFECTION

To get the intense mushroom flavour that is the keynote of this soup, you must cook the mushrooms until they reduce down to a fraction of their original size. This is the way to concentrate their flavour.

Tip the pile of raw mushrooms over the shallot and garlic mix. Don't worry if there seem to be too many mushrooms for the pan – they will start to shrink once cooking begins.

Stir the mushrooms several times during cooking, to make sure they cook evenly. Each time you stir you'll notice how they've shrunk down in the pan.

After simmering in stock, the mushrooms will have reduced down to a dark, juicy mass that covers the bottom of the pan.

CUCUMBER AND YOGURT GAZPACHO

When I'm staying in a hotel on holiday, I often order gazpacho, and it always amazes me how much it varies from one place to another. My version includes cucumber, horseradish, and dill – perfect partners that go naturally together in a salad, so why not in a soup?

SERVES 6-8
**3 cucumbers, finely sliced
(including the skin)**
**1/4 large bunch of fresh dill,
chopped with the stalks**
2tbsp bottled horseradish sauce
**750ml chilled Vegetable Nage
(below)**
300g natural Greek yogurt
**Sea salt and freshly milled
white pepper**

TO SERVE
Extra-virgin olive oil
**Very thin slices of focaccia
bread, lightly toasted**

Mix the cucumbers and dill in a bowl. Whisk the horseradish into the nage, season with salt, and mix with the cucumber and dill. Cover and marinate in the fridge overnight.

Liquidize the marinated ingredients in batches with the yogurt until smooth, adding a few twists of pepper. Transfer to a clean bowl. Place this in a larger bowl half filled with ice cubes and chill in the fridge for 2–3 hours.

When ready to serve, check and correct the seasoning of the soup, then ladle into chilled bowls. Garnish with droplets of olive oil, and accompany with toasted focaccia.

VEGETABLE NAGE
This needs to be made the day before required.

MAKES 750ML
**1 leek, outside leaves discarded,
cut into 3cm lengths**
**4 carrots, peeled and cut into
2cm lengths**
**2 white-skinned onions, each cut
lengthways into eighths**
**2 celery sticks, cut into 3cm
lengths**
**3 garlic cloves, peeled and
left whole**
1 star anise
1/2tsp coriander seeds
1/4tsp white peppercorns
**A handful of mixed fresh herbs,
including parsley, basil, chives,
and chervil**
3 lemon wedges
100ml dry white wine

Put the vegetables and garlic into a large, heavy pan. Pour in about 1 litre cold water – enough to reach the same level as the vegetables – and bring to the boil over a high heat. Skim off any froth, then turn the heat down to medium and simmer uncovered for exactly 8 minutes.

While the vegetables are simmering, crush the star anise with the coriander seeds and peppercorns.

As soon as the 8 minutes are up, add the crushed spices to the liquid together with the herbs and lemon wedges. Simmer uncovered for a further 2 minutes, then immediately take the pan off the heat and stir in the wine. Leave until cold.

Ladle the liquid and vegetables into a glass or plastic container, cover tightly, and refrigerate for 24 hours.

The next day, strain the liquid through a fine sieve. Discard the vegetables. Keep the nage covered in the fridge until ready to use.

KEY TO PERFECTION

For a delicate chilled soup, it is important to use the right liquid for the base flavour. Chicken or vegetable stock would be too strong, water too weak. Scented vegetable nage is the answer.

Spices, fresh herbs, and lemon wedges add their scent and flavour to the vegetables and liquid, but they should be heated for only 2 minutes or their freshness will be lost.

As soon as the nage is cold, decant it into a container and put it in the fridge. Don't let it sit out in the warm or the vegetables will become slimy.

Use the finest sieve you have for straining this delicate stock. The liquid should come through crystal clear.

ALL IS NOT LOST

If you think the soup isn't cold enough when you come to serve it, give it a chill boost by submerging a plastic bag of ice cubes in it for a few minutes.

**PLAN AHEAD BEFORE
YOU START COOKING**

*"Read the recipe from
start to finish, making
sure you understand
both the ingredients
and the method.
If you can do this
the day before, so
much the better."*

LEEK AND POTATO SOUP

One of the first classic recipes I learnt to cook, this soup makes a perfect dinner party starter. It looks elegant, and its delicate flavour won't clash with anything that comes after it. In the summer I serve it chilled and give it its French name, vichyssoise.

SERVES 6
5 large leeks (about 1kg in total)
2 King Edward potatoes
(about 400g in total)
150g unsalted butter
1 white-skinned onion,
finely sliced
3 garlic cloves, chopped
750ml boiling hot Chicken Stock
(page 16)
3–4tbsp double cream
Sea salt and freshly milled
white pepper

TO SERVE
6tbsp double cream
Finely snipped fresh chives

Cut off and discard the roots of the leeks and the dark green tops, leaving behind some of the light green. You should be left with 700–800g leeks to use. Cut them in half lengthways, then slice across into fine strips. Wash the strips well in cold water and drain. Peel the potatoes (you should have 300–350g to use after peeling) and rinse briefly. Cut into wedges and slice finely. Don't wash the slices – the potato starch will help thicken the soup.

Heat 100g of the butter in a large, heavy pan over a medium heat until foaming. Add the onion and garlic, and stir and cook without colouring for a couple of minutes until they start to soften. Add the leeks, season with salt, and stir well. Cover the pan tightly and cook over a medium-high heat for 8 minutes, stirring occasionally.

Mix the potatoes in with the leeks, then stir in the boiling stock a ladleful at a time. Immediately bring back to the boil, then cover and cook for a further 8 minutes until both potatoes and leeks are tender.

Working in batches, blitz the soup straightaway in a blender until smooth, adding the cream and the remaining butter in small pieces while the machine is running. Now pass the soup through a sieve into a clean pan and reheat gently without boiling.

Taste and correct the seasoning if necessary, and serve topped with a swirl of cream and a sprinkling of chives.

"You need just enough potatoes to give body to the leeks without making the soup floury and bland. Don't go by the number of vegetables alone – a successful marriage of leeks and potatoes is also judged by weight."

KEY TO PERFECTION

The hallmark of a good leek and potato soup is its velvety smoothness. Cooking the leeks and potatoes together to the same degree of softness is the secret behind this. Undercooked leeks will be stringy, and no amount of blending and sieving will get rid of this.

It is important to slice the potatoes very thinly so they cook in half the time it takes the leeks to become soft. If the potatoes are added too early they will overcook and become grainy; if they're added too late, the leeks will overcook before the potatoes are done.

By the time you add the potatoes, the leeks will be half cooked. They should be glossy and bright green.

With the help of a small ladle, perfectly cooked leeks and potatoes will pass freely through the sieve after blending. A conical sieve called a chinois makes the job easy because it allows you to press and rotate the ladle against the inside to push the vegetables through.

ROASTED VINE TOMATO SOUP

My boys love tomato soup, so I often make this at home. Served with crusty bread and cheese, it makes a complete meal, and it's so easy because it needs virtually no cooking. The great flavour comes from the combination of roasted fresh tomatoes and sun-dried tomatoes.

SERVES 4
150ml olive oil
½ small white-skinned onion, roughly chopped
3 garlic cloves, sliced
1kg over-ripe vine tomatoes
150g sun-dried tomatoes in oil
3 sprigs of fresh basil
3 sprigs of fresh coriander
2tbsp tomato purée
Worcestershire sauce, to taste
Balsamic vinegar, to taste
500ml hot Chicken Stock (page 16)
Sea salt and freshly milled black pepper

TO SERVE
Extra-virgin olive oil
Fresh basil leaves

Heat the oven to 220°C fan (240°C/gas 9). Heat a large roasting pan in the oven for 3–4 minutes. Pour the oil into the hot pan, then add the onion, garlic, and the whole tomatoes taken off the vine. Season and stir, then roast for 15 minutes.

Stir in the sun-dried tomatoes and their oil, and scatter the herbs over the top. Roast for a further 10 minutes, then mix in the tomato purée and roast for a final 5 minutes.

Tip the contents of the pan into a large bowl, add 2tbsp each Worcestershire sauce and balsamic vinegar, and stir well. Cover the bowl with cling film and leave to marinate for half an hour.

Blitz the soup in batches in a blender until smooth, then pass through a fine sieve into a pan. Heat to a simmer, then pour in the stock and stir well. Taste and correct the seasoning, adding up to 4tsp more Worcestershire sauce and 3tsp more balsamic vinegar, if you like.

Serve hot, topping each bowl with a drizzle of olive oil, some basil leaves, and freshly milled black pepper.

"Tomatoes love Worcestershire sauce – just think of a Bloody Mary. Here I've used balsamic vinegar as well. These two strong seasonings complement one another, and hold their own against the intense tomato flavour."

KEY TO PERFECTION

For the intense, smoky flavour that sets this soup apart from any other tomato soup, the secret is in the way the tomatoes are cooked.

Roast the vine tomatoes until they blister and burst. Don't worry if the sun-dried tomatoes are tinged with black. The skins are sieved out before serving, but the lovely smoky flavour will be left behind.

ALL IS NOT LOST

If you've been a little heavy handed with the seasonings and the soup tastes too powerful, you can whisk in a few small pieces of unsalted butter at the reheating stage. The butter will mellow the flavour, and take the edge off any sharpness.

CHUNKY CHICKEN SOUP

This is a very special chicken soup. Cooking the chicken in homemade stock concentrates the flavour, then using the stock to make a velouté sauce gives the soup a wonderful creamy consistency without adding cream. Served with hot crusty bread, it makes a great lunch or supper.

SERVES 6
1.5kg organic chicken
1.3 litres cold Chicken Stock (page 16)
2 large carrots, peeled and cut into 2cm dice
1 Spanish onion, cut into 2cm dice
2 celery sticks, strings removed and cut into 2cm dice
1 leek (white part only), cut into 2cm dice
2 garlic cloves, very finely chopped
100g unsalted butter
100g plain white flour
Sea salt and freshly milled black pepper

TO SERVE
Shavings of fresh Parmesan cheese
A small handful of finely shredded fresh flat-leaf parsley

Remove the string and any giblets from the chicken. Soak the bird in a bowl of cold water for 10 minutes, so there will be less scum on the surface of the stock.

Drain the chicken and put it in a large, heavy pan. Pour in the stock and about 2.5 litres cold water to cover the bird, then add a pinch of salt. Bring to the boil over a high heat. Immediately skim off any fat and scum, then turn the heat down and simmer uncovered for 1¼ hours. Remove from the heat and leave the chicken to cool in the liquid.

Lift out the bird. Strain the stock, measure 1.8 litres, and set aside; reserve the remaining stock for blanching the vegetables. Take the chicken meat from the bones, discarding all skin, veins, and sinew. Break the meat into large shreds with your fingers. Set aside.

Pour 500ml of the unmeasured stock into a medium pan, add a pinch of salt, and bring to the boil. Add the vegetables, bring back to the boil, and blanch for 2–3 minutes until just tender. Drain in a colander set over a bowl to catch the blanching liquid.

Mix the blanching liquid with the measured stock in a clean pan and bring to the boil. Add the garlic. Boil for 15–20 minutes to reduce to about 1.4 litres. Turn the heat down to low and keep the stock hot.

Make the velouté sauce in a large, heavy pan. Melt the butter over a medium-high heat, sprinkle in the flour, and stir to make a roux. Gradually beat and whisk in the reduced hot stock. Bring to the boil and simmer, whisking, for about 5 minutes.

Add the shredded chicken and vegetables to the sauce and heat through gently. Taste and correct the seasoning, and add a little extra stock if the soup is too thick. Serve topped with shavings of Parmesan, shredded parsley, and freshly milled pepper.

KEY TO PERFECTION

The best chicken soups have a silky consistency, which comes from making a smooth velouté sauce with the stock – the French word *velouté* means velvety.

Cook the butter and flour, stirring constantly with a wooden spoon, for 4–5 minutes until the mix becomes a light golden paste or roux. Don't skimp on the time – the flour must be thoroughly cooked or it will taste raw in the finished soup.

Add the stock to the roux a ladleful at a time, beating vigorously to blend it in after each addition. Beat with the spoon at first, then change to a whisk once the sauce becomes more liquid. This gradual addition of stock is the secret of a perfectly smooth sauce without lumps.

After simmering and whisking for 5 minutes, the flour will be thoroughly cooked and the sauce will have a velvety, pouring consistency.

FISH & SHELLFISH

SEARED TUNA

How you serve tuna is entirely up to you, but I prefer my tuna like this – seared on the outside, rare in the centre. When the fish is fresh I think it's the best way to get the most out of its delicate flavour.

SERVES 2
**2 x 175–200g tuna loin
steaks (preferably yellowfin),
each cut 2.5cm thick
Olive oil
Sea salt and cracked
white pepper**

Pat the fish with kitchen paper to remove any blood and condensation. The fish should be completely dry before cooking.

Put a non-stick frying pan over a high heat, splash in enough oil to cover the bottom thinly, and heat until hot. To check the oil is hot enough, hold your hand about 7cm above the pan – you should feel the heat rising on your palm.

Sprinkle the fish on one side only with salt and pepper. Place seasoned side down in the hot oil and sprinkle the top with salt and pepper. Turn the heat down to medium-high and leave undisturbed for about 2 minutes.

Flip the fish over with a palette knife, and cook undisturbed again for about 2 minutes. Remove the tuna to a board and leave to rest for a few minutes.

Working across the grain with a very sharp knife, cut each steak into 5mm-thick slices. Serve sprinkled with salt and pepper, and drizzled with olive oil if you like.

KEY TO PERFECTION

For the best results, let your eyes do the timing as well as the clock. Recipes that give precise cooking times will often disappoint because they can't know the exact degree of heat you use, nor the type of pan or precise thickness of the steak.

On the first side, watch the colour of the fish gradually change from the bottom of the steak until just below the halfway mark.

After flipping the fish, watch closely until the colour changes to just below the halfway mark again. There should be a thin stripe of uncooked tuna running through the centre.

ALL IS NOT LOST

If you haven't got a non-stick pan, or the one you've got has seen better days, you may find that the tuna sticks when the time comes to turn it over. Don't panic. Turn the heat up to high and leave the fish undisturbed for another minute or two until it gets well coloured on the bottom and cooked up to the top edge. Then baste it with the hot oil from the pan to colour the top. The underside will be crisp and dry, and the tuna will come away easily from the pan. The fish will be medium rather than rare, but it will look good – and it will be all in one piece.

"The thickness of the fish is important. If it's cut too thin it will overcook and be dry, but if it's too thick you'll find it difficult to get the centre right without overcooking the outside. Always buy tuna steak from the fishmonger, so you can get it cut to the exact thickness you want."

PAN-FRIED SCALLOPS

I love this recipe because it brings back happy memories of my time at Le Gavroche in London, where I had my first experience of cooking diver-caught scallops. I think this way of cooking scallops is the best – it brings out their natural sweetness.

SERVES 2
6 large fresh scallops, preferably diver caught
1tsp mild curry powder
1tsp fine salt
Olive oil
Lentils with Herbs (page 142), to serve

Remove the frilly skirts, muscles, and any corals from the scallops, then wash the scallops in cold water and drain well. Lay them flat on one half of a cloth draped over a tray and cover with the other half of the cloth. Leave to dry in the fridge overnight.

Mix the curry powder and salt together, sprinkle over a plate, and leave overnight (the mix needs to dry out or the salt might make the scallops damp).

When you're ready to cook, put a non-stick frying pan over a medium-high heat. Splash in enough olive oil to cover the bottom of the pan thinly and heat until very hot.

Cut the scallops in half. Sprinkle half of the pieces with curry salt, then fry for about 20 seconds on each side. Drain on kitchen paper while cooking the rest of the scallops in the same way. Serve immediately, with the lentils.

"The drier the scallops are, the better – leaving them to dry out in the fridge overnight really helps with the cooking. This is especially beneficial with dredged scallops, most of which are very watery because they have been frozen and then defrosted."

KEY TO PERFECTION

The scallops must not be overcooked. To be sure they cook quickly and evenly, they should all be the same size, and each one should be in the hot frying pan for the same amount of time.

Stand each scallop up, holding it between your forefinger and thumb. Squeeze until you feel the flesh firm up, then make a clean slice through the centre with a very sharp knife. You will now have 12 pieces that are all of a similar thickness.

Wait 10 seconds after putting the last one in, then sprinkle each scallop with curry salt and turn it over, starting with the one that went into the pan first and working clockwise. By the time you get to the last scallop, the first one will be ready to be removed.

Put 6 pieces of scallop on the fingertips, thumb, and heel of one hand, and sprinkle them with curry salt. Starting with the one on the heel of your hand, and working from 12 o'clock in a clockwise direction, put them seasoned side down in the hot frying pan in a semicircle.

GRIDDLED SALMON

Fish that is griddled correctly should have two textures – a crust on the outside and a rare centre that is beautifully moist and soft. This gives you the best of both worlds, and is cooked exactly how I like it.

SERVES 4
4 x 200g centre-cut (thick) salmon fillet portions, without skin
Olive oil, for drizzling
Sea salt and freshly milled black pepper
Bittersweet Chicory Salad (page 114), to serve

Neaten each piece of salmon by trimming off any ragged edges. Pat the fish dry, making sure there are no traces of blood.

Put a dry griddle pan over a high heat until it is very hot. Drizzle the top (presentation) side of each fillet with olive oil and sprinkle with salt and pepper.

Turn the heat down to medium-high and put the salmon in the pan, laying it diagonally across the ridges with its presentation side down. Cook for 1½ minutes until seared underneath, then rotate the pieces in the opposite direction and cook for another 1½ minutes. Now turn the pieces over and cook for a further 3 minutes.

To serve, divide the salad among four plates, reserving a little of the dressing. Put the salmon on top of the salad, sprinkle with pepper, and drizzle over the reserved dressing.

KEY TO PERFECTION

To get distinct chargrilled lines on fish so that it looks barbecued, you must let the fish sit still while it's cooking. Don't be tempted to shake the pan or move the fish, or you won't get an imprint of charred lines. Shaking the pan will also slow down the cooking, and moving or prodding the fish will release juices and make the fish watery – all the more reason not to do it.

After cooking for 3 minutes, first searing the fish in one direction and then the other, turn the pieces over to reveal the diamond pattern on the presentation side. Continue cooking for another 3 minutes without moving the fish – there is no need for a charred pattern on the skinned side of the fish as it will not be seen.

PAN-FRIED SEA BASS

I learnt how to prepare sea bass at The Savoy – the fish was the first professional section I worked on after leaving college. I used to fillet and score fish day in, day out, but that was as far as it went. Only when I got to Le Gavroche did I actually start cooking fish, and it was there I learnt that the simpler you do it, the better.

SERVES 4
1 whole sea bass, weighing 1.1–1.35kg, scaled, cleaned, and cut into 2 long fillets (ask the fishmonger to do this)
Olive oil
Sea salt and freshly milled white pepper

Check for tiny pin bones in the flesh side of the fish and pull them out if you find any. Turn the fish over and score the skin, then cut each fillet in half crossways to make four portions altogether. Season the scored skin with a little salt and pepper.

Put a large, non-stick frying pan over a high heat, splash in enough oil to cover the bottom thinly, and heat until hot.

Lower the heat to medium-high, put in the fish skin side down, and cook undisturbed for 4 minutes until the skin is crisp and golden. Don't shake the pan or move the fillets as this will cause moisture to come out of the fish – then the skin will stick to the pan and tear. If the pan gets too hot, draw it to the side of the heat and pour in a little cold oil to cool it down, then return it to the heat.

Turn the fish over and cook undisturbed for 2 minutes on the second side, basting with the hot oil so that it runs into the crevices in the skin.

To serve, place the sea bass skin side up on four plates and drizzle over the pan juices. Dust with white pepper if you like.

"I like pan-frying sea bass for a quick supper. It goes with lots of things – a mixed leaf or chicory salad, pasta or rice, or Jersey Royals tossed in freshly made mint sauce."

KEY TO PERFECTION

The skin of sea bass must be scored so the fish will stay flat during cooking. If the fish isn't flat, it won't cook evenly, and you won't be able to tell if it's done or not.

At the end of the cooking time, turn each piece of fish over onto its skin side again. Push down on the fish with your fingertips and hold them there for 10–15 seconds. The fish is ready when it feels firm, not spongy, and it should be removed from the hot pan straightaway.

With a very sharp, large knife and a sawing action, cut diagonal slashes through the skin of each fillet. Make the score lines close together, and cut right through the skin just into the fish.

ALL IS NOT LOST

If you haven't scored the skin properly, or you've forgotten to score it at all, the fish will curl at the edges as soon as it goes in the pan, and then it won't cook evenly. Quickly press it hard with a spatula to force it down flat. You'll find it quite powerful and strong, so you'll need to use some force.

CLAM CHOWDER

I used to make chowder like this when I worked at The Point, a luxury resort in upstate New York. We served it in a large tureen on the terrace at lunchtime – the guests helped themselves and ate it while enjoying the view of the beautiful Adirondack mountains.

SERVES 4

1.5kg fresh live clams (palourdes or amandes)
150g unsalted butter
40g plain white flour
200ml dry white wine
750ml hot Fish Stock (opposite)
150g fresh sweetcorn kernels or drained and rinsed canned sweetcorn
1 Spanish onion, finely diced
1 leek (white part only), cut into 1cm dice
2 garlic cloves, finely chopped
1 large King Edward potato (about 200g), peeled and cut into 1cm dice
150ml double cream
A handful of fresh parsley (curly or flat-leaf), roughly chopped
Sea salt and freshly milled white pepper

Soak the clams in cold water for at least 20 minutes, or up to an hour, to clean them.

Meanwhile, make a beurre manié (butter and flour *liaison*). Soften 50g of the butter and mix in the flour to make a thick paste. Keep in the fridge until ready to use.

Drain the clams in a colander, rinse under the cold tap to check there's no sand left in the shells, and drain again. Discard any clams that are open or that do not close when tapped sharply on the worktop. Heat a wide pan over a high heat until hot, tip in the clams and wine, and cover the pan tightly. Give the pan a shake, then take off the lid – some or all of the clams will be open. Remove the open ones with a slotted spoon and set aside. Put the lid on again, and continue until all the clams have opened. (Discard any that stay closed.)

When the clams are cool enough to handle, remove them from their shells, reserving some in shells for the garnish. Pour the cooking liquid slowly through a fine sieve into a clean pan, leaving the sediment behind in the bottom of the first pan. Mix the hot fish stock with the cooking liquid and set aside.

If using fresh sweetcorn, blanch it in a small pan of salted boiling water for 1 minute, then drain and rinse under the cold tap.

Heat the remaining butter in a heavy pan over a medium heat. Add the onion, leek, and garlic, and cook without colouring for a few minutes until they start to soften. Season with a little salt. Add the potato and cook for about 5 minutes until softened, then remove from the heat and stir in the shelled clams and sweetcorn. Set aside.

Bring the fish stock to the boil. Whisk in the beurre manié in small pieces, then boil and whisk until thickened. Stir in the cream and bring back to the boil, then add the clams and vegetables and heat through gently for a minute or two. Season lightly, and finish by adding the clams in their shells and the parsley. Serve hot.

FISH STOCK

MAKES ABOUT 1.5 LITRES
1.5kg white fish bones with heads (from sole, plaice, halibut, or turbot), gills and eyes removed
5tbsp olive oil
1 Spanish onion, cut into 3cm dice
1 leek (white part only), cut into 3cm dice
2 celery sticks, cut into 3cm dice
1 bulb garlic, cut crossways in half
10 coriander seeds
5 white peppercorns
300ml dry white wine

Cut the fish bones into 6cm pieces. Soak in cold water for 10 minutes, then drain in a colander.

Heat the oil in a large, heavy pan. Add the vegetables, garlic, and spices, and stir, then cook over a low heat for 5 minutes until the vegetables start to soften. Pour in the wine. Increase the heat, bring to the boil, and reduce for 2 minutes.

Add the fish bones and 1.5 litres cold water. Bring to the boil over a high heat, then immediately turn down to a gentle simmer and shake the pan gently – most of the impurities will rise to the top. Skim off the scum with a ladle, then bring the stock back up to a moderate simmer. Cook for 20 minutes, skimming off any impurities as they appear.

Strain the stock through a colander set over a bowl. Discard the bones and vegetables, then strain the stock through a fine sieve into a clean pan or bowl. Use the stock straightaway, or cool quickly and refrigerate in a covered container.

"Palourdes and amandes are small types of clam that tend to be more tender than the larger types. You can use larger clams, such as cherrystones, but you will need to cook them for a few minutes longer initially and then cut the meat into small pieces. Cockles make a good alternative to clams."

KEY TO PERFECTION

The liquid in a chowder should be like velvet, and there are two ways to achieve this. You should remove all the sand and grit from the clams before you start cooking, then use a butter and flour *liaison* (beurre manié) at the end to thicken the liquid and give it a smooth consistency. Classic recipes thicken the chowder once everything is in, but it's better to thicken the stock on its own so you don't crush the delicate potatoes and clams.

Whisk the beurre manié into the boiling liquid a teaspoon at a time, letting it dissolve before adding the next amount.

Leave the clams to soak in a large bowl of cold water for up to an hour before you use them, moving them around with your hands now and again. The colder the water the better, or the clams might start to open, so add a few ice cubes to cool it down. Change the water a few times to check on the amount of sand that's still emerging from the clams.

Once all the beurre manié is in and the stock has thickened, continue boiling and whisking for a few minutes to cook the flour, or it will taste raw in the chowder. At the end of this time, the liquid will be velvety smooth.

SOLE WITH CAPER AND LEMON BUTTER

This simple, classic favourite is one of the most popular dishes on the menu at the Savoy Grill. There we make it with Dover sole, but at home I use lemon sole, which is easier to get hold of and less expensive.

SERVES 2
2 x 500g whole lemon sole, gutted, and heads, tails, and skin removed (ask the fishmonger to do this)
85g plain white flour, seasoned with salt and pepper
3tbsp olive oil
Sea salt and freshly milled black pepper

FOR THE CAPER AND LEMON BUTTER
50g unsalted butter
50g small capers
Juice of ½ lemon
2tbsp roughly chopped fresh curly parsley

Dredge the fish in seasoned flour.

Put a large, non-stick frying pan over a high heat, pour in the oil, and heat until hot. Place the fish in the oil and shake the pan to be sure that the fish isn't sticking to it. Leave to cook undisturbed for 4 minutes until golden brown underneath, then turn the fish over and cook for a further 4 minutes undisturbed.

While the fish is cooking, make the caper and lemon butter. Heat a small, non-stick frying pan over a medium-high heat, add the butter, and wait until it starts to foam. Now stir the butter with a wooden spoon until the foam starts to drop and turn nut brown. Quickly stir in the capers followed by the lemon juice and chopped parsley. Stir vigorously all the time. Remove from the heat and keep hot.

As soon as the fish is done, transfer it to plates and spoon over the hot caper and lemon butter.

"In a restaurant you can ask for fish to be taken off the bone, but this would be stress beyond belief to do at home – the fish would be stone cold by the time you got it to the table. Cooked as it is here, it's very easy to just lift the fish off the bone on your plate with a knife and fork."

KEY TO PERFECTION

Sole is delicate and can quickly overcook and become dry. Coating the fish with flour and pan-frying it whole on the bone is the best way to get moist flesh with a just-cooked flavour. You also need to know the right moment to remove the fish from the pan.

Spread the flour out on a tray and season with salt and pepper. Dip each fish in the flour until thickly and evenly coated on both sides, then pat and shake off the excess.

The side of the fish that was cooked first will be an even golden colour when the fish is turned over. This is the flour that has formed a protective coating against the hot oil, preventing the fish from overcooking.

To check the fish is done, tease the flesh away from the bone with a palette knife at the thickest point along the central line. Perfectly cooked fish will come away from the bone easily, without scraping or tugging.

FISH PIE

Just about everyone loves fish pie, and my wife, Jane, makes the best. When I make it, I like to include tiger prawns because they add texture to the soft white fish, and they have such a well-defined shellfish flavour. Sometimes I use cockles, mussels, or shrimps for a change. Another favourite combination is smoked haddock with white fish and prawns.

SERVES 4
300ml cold Fish Stock (page 45)
2 small sprigs of fresh thyme
1 bay leaf, cut in half
2 celery sticks, strings removed and finely diced
1 small white-skinned onion, cut into 2cm dice
1 leek (white part only), cut crossways into 1cm rounds
10 raw tiger prawns in their shells
400ml full-fat milk, plus a little extra if needed
500g skinless, thick white fish fillets (eg cod or haddock), cut into 3cm cubes
Leaves of 1 small bunch of fresh flat-leaf parsley, coarsely chopped
600ml hot Béchamel Sauce (opposite)
Sea salt and freshly milled white pepper

FOR THE TOPPING
1 quantity hot Mash (page 98)
2 large organic egg yolks
1 whole nutmeg, for grating

Pour the stock into a medium saucepan and add 1 sprig of thyme, a piece of bay leaf, and some salt and pepper. Bring to the boil over a high heat. Add the vegetables and turn down the heat to medium. Simmer uncovered for 8–10 minutes until tender, then remove from the heat. With a slotted spoon, transfer the vegetables to a colander set over a bowl. Drain the vegetables, then dry well. Pour the drained-off liquid into the stock in the pan and reserve.

Peel the prawns and halve lengthways. Remove any black veins and rinse the prawns briefly under the cold tap. Bring the stock back to the boil and drop in the prawns. Cover and simmer for 1 1/2 minutes until they all turn pink. Remove the prawns with a slotted spoon, drain, and dry well. Reserve the stock.

Next cook the fish. Bring the milk to the boil in a clean pan with the remaining thyme and bay leaf and some salt and pepper. Add the fish and bring back to the boil, then take off the heat and leave to stand for 4–5 minutes. Remove the fish with a slotted spoon, drain, and dry well. Strain the reserved stock and milk into a measuring jug and make up to 600ml with more milk if necessary. Use for the béchamel sauce.

Gently mix the vegetables, prawns, and fish together, then divide among four individual ovenproof dishes (or use one large baking dish). Sprinkle with the parsley, then gradually ladle the hot béchamel sauce on top until it reaches the same level as the filling. Don't mix the sauce through or it will break up the fish.

Heat the oven to 180°C fan (200°C/gas 6). Place the ovenproof dishes or baking dish on a baking tray.

Beat the mash with the egg yolks and cool slightly, then pipe on top of the fish mixture using a 1cm plain nozzle. Grate nutmeg evenly over the top. Bake for 20–25 minutes (about 35 minutes for a large pie) until the potato topping is tinged golden brown and the filling is bubbling. Serve hot.

BÉCHAMEL SAUCE

MAKES ABOUT 600ML
50g unsalted butter
50g plain white flour
600ml mixed milk and stock
(from Fish Pie, opposite)
4tbsp double cream
Sea salt and freshly milled
white pepper

This recipe uses a combination of milk and fish stock, because this gives a good flavour to the fish pie; a basic béchamel sauce is made with milk only.

Melt the butter in a heavy pan over a medium-high heat until it is foaming. Sprinkle in the flour and stir constantly for 3–4 minutes until you have a light golden paste or roux. Add the milk and stock to the roux in five stages, beating and whisking until smooth before adding the next stage. When all the liquid has been incorporated, turn the heat down to low and cook for a further 6–8 minutes, whisking regularly. Remove from the heat, stir in the cream, and add seasoning to taste.

KEY TO PERFECTION

The vegetables, prawns, and fish must be completely dry before they are mixed with the sauce. If they are wet, they will dilute the sauce and make the pie watery.

In turn, as they are cooked, spread the drained vegetables, prawns, and fish out on a clean, dry cloth (or sheets of kitchen paper) and pat them thoroughly dry.

STEAMED COD WITH PERFUMED BROTH

I always associate steamed fish with the bland food that people eat when they're not well or on a diet. This recipe is the exact opposite of that, because it adds flavour to the fish in the most fantastic way. When you smell the aromas of the broth wafting through your kitchen, you'll know exactly what I mean.

SERVES 2
1 large bunch of fresh basil
2 x 200g cod fillets, with skin on
Extra-virgin olive oil, for drizzling
Sea salt and freshly milled
black pepper

FOR THE BROTH
30 coriander seeds
20 white peppercorns
1 star anise
1tbsp sea salt
500ml cold Fish Stock (page 45)
500ml cold Vegetable Nage
(page 22)
3 stems of lemongrass, roughly
sliced on the diagonal
Pared zest and juice of 2 lemons
20 sprigs of fresh coriander
10 sprigs of fresh basil
10 sprigs of fresh flat-leaf parsley

First make the broth. Crush the spices and salt together with a knife or in a mortar and pestle. Put them in a pan that is the same diameter as your steamer basket and add the remaining broth ingredients. Bring to the boil over a high heat, then cover the pan and boil the broth for 10 minutes. This will get the scent going so the broth will impart flavour to the fish.

Make a bed of basil leaves in the steamer basket. Season and oil the fish well, then nestle the fillets in the basil and put the lid on the basket. Place it on top of the pan of boiling broth, turn the heat down to a brisk simmer, and steam for 8 minutes until the skin will peel easily off the fish.

Serve the hot cod skinned, sprinkled with sea salt and freshly milled pepper and drizzled with olive oil.

"Be generous with the amount of salt you sprinkle on the skin. You're not going to eat it, because the skin is coming off, but the flavour will permeate the fish like cooking in a salt crust."

KEY TO PERFECTION

Like many other white fish, cod has a flaky texture and a tendency to fall apart. Gentle steaming is one of the best ways to cook it, and leaving the skin on helps hold it together.

Season the fish and fold in half with the skin on the outside, then sprinkle generously with salt and drizzle with olive oil before placing in the basil-lined steamer. As the fish cooks, the skin will act as a natural protective layer over the delicate flesh.

With your fingers, carefully peel away the skin to reveal the juicy, perfectly cooked white fish underneath. Throw away the skin before serving – steamed skin is flabby, so not good to eat.

SALT AND PEPPER PRAWNS

Tiger prawns and soft-shell crabs are my favourite starters when I go out for a Chinese meal, and it's hard to choose between them. These prawns in tempura batter are easy to make at home – and they're great to serve as canapés with drinks.

SERVES 4
16 raw tiger prawns
in their shells
85g plain white flour
Vegetable oil, for deep-frying
Sea salt and finely cracked
black pepper

FOR THE TEMPURA BATTER
50g plain white flour
50g cornflour
1/4 tsp bicarbonate of soda
150ml ice-cold sparkling water
2 ice cubes
1 large organic egg white, lightly
whisked until frothy

TO SERVE
2tsp Thai sweet chilli sauce,
or to taste
4tbsp good-quality mayonnaise
1 red chilli, deseeded and
finely chopped
2 spring onions, finely chopped

First make a dip to serve with the prawns by mixing the chilli sauce into the mayonnaise. Keep in a covered bowl in the fridge.

Peel the prawns and cut in half lengthways. Remove any black veins, then rinse briefly under the cold tap. Don't worry if the prawns are wet – this will help the flour stick.

Spread the flour out on a tray, sprinkle with a little salt and plenty of pepper, and stir well to mix. Toss the prawns in the seasoned flour until evenly coated, then shake off the excess.

Make the tempura batter by sifting the flour, cornflour, and bicarbonate of soda into a bowl. Add the water, ice, and egg white, and whisk gently just to mix. Season with a little salt.

Heat oil in a wok or deep-fat fryer to 170ºC. To test the oil without a thermometer, dip a prawn in the batter and drop into the hot oil – if the batter crisps up within 2–3 minutes, the oil is hot enough.

Drop about one-third of the prawns into the batter and stir gently to coat, then take them out with a slotted spoon and lower them one at a time into the hot oil. Deep-fry for 2–3 minutes until the batter becomes crisp and light golden. Lift out with a slotted spoon and drain on kitchen paper while frying the remaining prawns in two batches.

Serve sprinkled with sea salt, chopped chilli, and spring onions, with the bowl of chilli mayo on the side.

"Don't try to deep-fry all the prawns at once. This will lower the temperature of the oil and the batter will not crisp up."

KEY TO PERFECTION

Sparkling water and bicarbonate of soda make tempura batter as light as air.
The secret is to work fast and not overmix, or you'll knock out the sparkle.

Add the water and ice cubes to the dry ingredients and immediately start whisking. You need to mix everything together as quickly as possible.

Whisk just until the ingredients come together. Don't try to whisk the lumps out – they will disappear when the batter is cooked.

SHOP FOR FRESH INGREDIENTS ON THE DAY

"Buy only as much as you need, and take time to source the best."

FISH CAKES

When I was young I absolutely hated fish cakes, but my opinion changed when I started eating out in London in my twenties and had them at The Ivy. I've perfected this recipe over the years, to make a fish cake that is soft and fluffy and crab-flavoured inside, with a crisp and crunchy coating.

SERVES 4
300g cod or haddock fillet, skin on
Olive oil, for drizzling
300g fresh white crab meat, picked over to remove all shell and patted dry
Leaves of 1 small bunch of fresh flat-leaf parsley, finely chopped
100ml Fish Stock (page 45)
100ml double cream
2 shallots, very finely diced
1 celery stick, strings removed and very finely diced
1/2 leek (white part only), very finely diced
3 large King Edward potatoes (about 500g in total), peeled and cut into 2cm dice
Vegetable oil, for shallow frying
Sea salt and freshly milled white pepper

FOR THE COATING
100g plain white flour, seasoned with salt and pepper
2 large organic eggs, beaten
175g natural dried breadcrumbs (from a packet)

Heat the oven to 170°C fan (190°C/gas 5). Put the fish skin side down on an oiled baking tray, season, and drizzle with a little olive oil. Roast for 10 minutes until the fish flakes easily but remains moist. Leave to cool, then take off the skin. Check there are no bones before flaking the fish and mixing with the crab meat and parsley.

Boil the stock in a pan until reduced by half. Add the cream and bring back to the boil, then reduce to a thick coating consistency (about 4tbsp), stirring often. Leave to cool, covered with cling film.

Heat a little olive oil in another pan and soften the shallots, celery, and leek for 4–5 minutes without colouring. Season, then cool on kitchen paper. Add the vegetables to the fish.

Put the potatoes in a pan of cold salted water over a high heat. Bring to the boil, then turn the heat down, cover, and simmer gently (don't boil) for 15–20 minutes until soft. Drain the potatoes, tip into a large bowl, and crush with a fork. Cool, then gently fold through the fish mixture followed by the cooled reduced sauce, a little at a time. Cover the bowl with cling film and refrigerate for at least an hour.

Form the mixture into eight cakes, then make them neater if you like by shaping them with a 9–10cm pastry cutter. Refrigerate for at least 10 minutes to firm up the shape, then coat in the seasoned flour, beaten eggs, and breadcrumbs. Refrigerate again for at least 10 minutes, to firm up the coating.

Heat 1cm vegetable oil in a non-stick frying pan over a high heat until hot. Pan-fry the fish cakes for 4 minutes on each side, basting frequently with the hot oil. Lift out with a fish slice, drain, and serve sprinkled with sea salt.

"Be gentle when mixing the fish, potatoes, and sauce together. You want a nice chunky mixture, not a purée."

KEY TO PERFECTION

Fish cakes won't hold together during frying if there's too much moisture in the mixture, so you must get the crab and potatoes really dry before combining them with the vegetables and sauce. Then you need to have a thick coating of breadcrumbs to seal everything in.

Crab is always wet, so spread it out on a cloth and pat it thoroughly dry. You can use a tea towel or kitchen paper, whichever you prefer.

When draining the diced potatoes, shake the colander and keep turning the potatoes over with a spoon so they become dry and fluffy.

Coat the cakes in a thick layer of breadcrumbs after dusting with flour and dipping in egg. These three layers form a protective coating around the soft fish and potato mixture during cooking, which helps prevent the fish cakes from breaking up.

MEAT

ROAST RIB OF BEEF

Sunday's the one day in the week I'm at home, and I love doing a roast lunch when friends and family come over. I was brought up on meat that was overcooked because my dad liked it done to death, but now I always cook it rare. That seems to suit most people, although when Dad's around, I carve off the first couple of slices for him – he cannot bear meat with any trace of blood.

SERVES 8
1 rib of beef joint with 4 bones, weighing about 5.8kg, boned and weighing about 4.6kg after boning (ask the butcher for the bones and get him to chop them)
3tbsp vegetable oil
Sea salt and cracked black pepper

FOR THE GRAVY
1 large Spanish onion, roughly chopped
2 carrots, peeled and roughly chopped
2 celery sticks, roughly chopped
2 garlic cloves, lightly crushed
A few sprigs of fresh or dried thyme
75g plain white flour
1 litre hot Beef Stock (page 11)

The beef should be at room temperature when it is put into the oven, so take it out of the fridge 1–2 hours before cooking.

Heat the oven to 180°C fan (200°C/gas 6).

Score the fat on top of the beef in a close diamond pattern, using a very sharp knife. Season the joint well on all sides. Heat the oil in a very large, heavy roasting pan over a high heat on top of the stove and sear the joint until evenly browned on all sides.

Remove the meat from the pan. Put the chopped bones in the pan, then sit the joint on top with the fat side up.

Roast the beef for 2 hours, basting well every 15 minutes, until a meat thermometer registers 60°C in the thickest part of the meat.

Transfer the meat to a board, cover loosely with foil, and leave to rest in a warm place for 25–30 minutes.

Make the gravy while the meat is resting. Carefully transfer the contents of the pan to a colander, leaving behind about 1tsp fat in the pan. Put the pan over a high heat on top of the stove. Add the vegetables, garlic, and thyme, and colour for about 5 minutes, then return the drained bones to the pan and sprinkle with the flour. Turn the bones to make sure they're well coated. Cook for about 5 minutes to colour the flour, then pour in about one-third of the hot stock and bubble to reduce. Pour in the remaining stock, stir well, and bring to the boil. Simmer until reduced to the consistency you like. Strain through a colander, then taste and adjust the seasoning.

Slice the beef thickly and put the slices overlapping on a warmed platter. Ladle over some of the gravy and serve the rest separately.

KEY TO PERFECTION

Roast beef should be crisp and well coloured on the outside, juicy and deep pink within. To get this perfect result, the secret is to sear it at the beginning of cooking.

ALL IS NOT LOST

If the bones are too darkly coloured at the end of cooking the meat, you can't use them to make gravy because they will make it taste bitter. For a quick fix, throw the bones away and use a clean pan to colour the vegetables in olive oil, then boost the flavour by pouring in about 100ml red wine and reduce before adding the stock.

Get the oil in the pan really hot, then put in the joint with its fat side facing down. Leave undisturbed until well coloured underneath, then turn the joint on one of its sides and baste with the hot oil. Leave undisturbed again, until the second side is coloured.

Repeat the turning, basting, and searing until the whole joint is browned on all four sides and the two ends. The total searing time should be about 20 minutes.

"The chopped bones from the joint make a natural trivet for the meat to roast on, as well as giving flavour to the gravy."

ROAST CHICKEN

I learnt this way of cooking a perfect roast chicken at Guy Savoy in Paris. There they used *poulet de Bresse*, considered the king of chickens in France for its gamey flavour and succulent meat. You can get *poulet de Bresse* here at good butchers and supermarkets, but if you can't get hold of one, buy an organic or free-range bird.

SERVES 4
1 chicken, preferably a *poulet de Bresse*, weighing about 1.5kg
2 red-skinned onions, quartered lengthways
2 white-skinned onions, quartered lengthways
4 carrots, peeled and cut into chunks
1 bulb garlic, cut crossways in half
A few sprigs of fresh or dried thyme
1 unwaxed lemon, cut lengthways into wedges
100ml olive oil
30 fresh sage leaves, finely sliced
750ml hot Chicken Stock (page 16)
20g cornflour (optional)
Sea salt and freshly milled black pepper

Heat the oven to 200°C fan (220°C/gas 7).

Remove any string and giblets from the chicken, then wipe the cavity clean with kitchen paper, and season inside with a good pinch of salt and a few twists of pepper. Put the onions, carrots, garlic, thyme, and lemon wedges in a roasting pan, season with salt and pepper, and stir in half the olive oil.

Sit the chicken breast-side up on top of the vegetables. Drizzle over the rest of the olive oil and sprinkle with salt and pepper. Roast for 1 hour 20 minutes, turning the bird regularly and basting with the cooking juices.

To check if the chicken is done, insert a skewer or the tip of a sharp, narrow-bladed knife deep into the thick end of a thigh. The bird is cooked if the juices run clear; if there are any traces of blood you will need to carry on cooking until they are gone.

When the chicken is cooked, transfer it to a board and cover loosely with foil. Leave to rest in a warm place for 10–15 minutes.

Remove the garlic, thyme, and lemon from the vegetables, then transfer the vegetables to a bowl with a slotted spoon and stir the sage leaves through them. Keep warm.

Strain the cooking liquid from the roasting pan into a saucepan. Pour in the stock and bring to the boil, then simmer until reduced to about 600ml. If you would like a thicker sauce, mix the cornflour to a paste with 2tbsp cold water, pour it into the pan, and boil for a few minutes, whisking constantly until thickened. Taste and adjust the seasoning, then pour the sauce into a jug.

Carve the chicken and serve with the vegetables and sauce.

"Use the vegetables to prop the chicken up when it's roasting on its side. This will stop it tumbling over."

KEY TO PERFECTION

For juicy, melt-in-the-mouth chicken, you need to turn the bird over several times and baste it well during roasting. This helps the heat penetrate evenly and makes the meat moist.

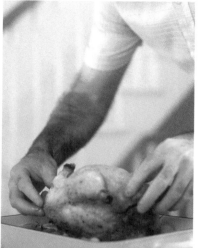

After the chicken has been roasting for half an hour, and the skin on the breast is nicely coloured and crisp, turn the bird onto one of its sides and baste well. Roast for 10 minutes, then turn the bird onto its other side. Baste and return to the oven to roast for another 10 minutes.

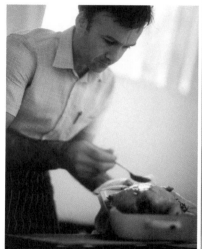

Now turn the chicken over onto its breast, so the back is facing up, and baste well. Return to the oven to roast for another 10 minutes. Finally, sit the bird breast-side up and roast for the remainder of the time.

GRIDDLED LAMB CHOPS

The griddle pan wasn't around when I was growing up, but I couldn't manage without one now. It's the perfect way to cook chops and steaks because the meat sits on the ridges of the pan and the fat runs into the grooves in between. This has to be healthier than letting the meat sit in its own fat during cooking.

SERVES 2
6–8 loin lamb chops
Olive oil, for brushing
1 small bunch of fresh rosemary
Sea salt and freshly milled black pepper

FOR THE MINT SAUCE
1tbsp redcurrant jelly
3tbsp malt vinegar
15g fresh mint leaves, finely chopped

TO SERVE
Spinach with Garlic and Cream (page 108)

First make the mint sauce. Melt the jelly over a low heat in a small pan. Remove from the heat and stir in the vinegar. Leave to cool before adding the mint. Use the sauce as soon as possible (within an hour of making it) or the mint will discolour.

Brush the meat lightly with olive oil. Season the fat and meat with salt and pepper.

Heat a dry griddle pan over a high heat until very hot. Put the chops fat side down in the pan and cook for 4–5 minutes until the fat renders and becomes crisp.

Lay the chops flat on one of their sides and strew the rosemary sprigs all over the meat. Cook for another 4–5 minutes, basting frequently with the fat in the pan.

Turn the chops over and cook the other sides for the same length of time, basting as before.

Serve the chops on a bed of spinach, with the mint sauce in a small bowl.

KEY TO PERFECTION

Rendering the fat in a griddle pan at the beginning of cooking will give the chops a crisp edge, then you can use the melted fat for basting the meat as it continues to cook. This will make the meat naturally moist and juicy, without the need for a lot of extra oil or fat.

Using tongs, stand the chops on their fat edges in the griddle pan, leaning them against the sides and each other for support. As the fat melts, it will run down between the ridges of the pan.

ROAST BELLY OF PORK
WITH CRACKLING

It used to be that when you did roast pork, you just scored the skin, rubbed it with salt, and put it straight in the oven. You'd get perfect crackling every time. These days, pork is bred leaner, so it isn't quite as easy. If you want good crackling, you need to take extra care.

SERVES 6
1 piece of boneless pork belly, weighing about 2kg, skin finely scored on the diagonal across its width (ask the butcher to do this)
20g fine salt
2 Spanish onions, cut lengthways into wedges
3 Granny Smith apples, cut lengthways into wedges and cores removed
1/2 bunch of fresh thyme
Olive oil, for drizzling
Sea salt and freshly milled white pepper

Trim off and discard any excess fat from the underside of the belly. Wipe the skin thoroughly dry, then rub half the fine salt into the skin and in between the score lines. Set aside for about 30 minutes.

Heat the oven to 160°C fan (180°C/gas 4).

Put the onion and apple wedges in a heavy roasting pan along with the thyme, a drizzle of oil, and a good sprinkling of salt and pepper. Put the pork on top of the onions and apples and wipe the skin dry again. Sprinkle the remaining fine salt over the skin and drizzle with oil. Massage these in well, then sprinkle with sea salt.

Place the roasting pan in the hottest part of the oven and roast for 1½ hours. Increase the temperature to 190°C fan (210°C/gas 6½) and roast for a further 45 minutes to 1 hour until the crackling is crisp. Remove the pork from the oven and allow to rest in a warm place for about 15 minutes.

Remove the crackling and cut into thin strips, then carve the meat crossways into neat slices. Serve the pork and crackling on warmed plates, with some of the roasted onion and apple.

"Crisp crackling comes from two sorts of salt. Fine salt brings out the moisture, then coarse sea salt creates a nice crust."

KEY TO PERFECTION

Pork has less fat and is wetter than it used to be, which makes it more difficult to get crisp crackling. Asking the butcher to finely score the joint will help overcome this, as will drying and salting the skin.

Pat the skin thoroughly dry with a clean cloth or a wad of kitchen paper. When the scored skin is dry, it will blister and crisp in the heat of the oven.

Sprinkle fine salt over the skin, then rub it into both the skin and the incisions. The salt will draw water out of the joint so that after it's been standing for half an hour you'll see beads of moisture collecting on the skin's surface.

ALL IS NOT LOST

If your crackling isn't quite crisp enough at the end of roasting, remove it from the pork in one piece, turn it upside down on a board, and scrape off the fat beneath using a spoon. Put it roasted side up on a baking tray lined with greaseproof paper and place in the hottest part of the oven to crisp for about 10 minutes.

BEEF HOTPOT

This is a combination of Lancashire hotpot and beef stew. I made my version of hotpot with lamb in individual dishes for the Great British Menu programme on television, and afterwards I thought, why not do it with beef? It works really well.

SERVES 6

1.5kg chuck steak, diced
About 150g plain white flour, seasoned with salt and pepper, for coating
Olive oil, for frying
1 Spanish onion, finely sliced
2 carrots, peeled and finely sliced
1 garlic clove, finely sliced
1 litre hot Beef Stock (page 11)
2tbsp fresh thyme leaves
3–4 medium to large King Edward or Maris Piper potatoes (about 700g total weight)
50g unsalted butter, melted
Sea salt and freshly milled black pepper

Heat the oven to 160°C fan (180°C/gas 4).

Coat the meat with seasoned flour. Put a large, deep non-stick frying pan over a high heat. Pour in enough oil just to cover the bottom of the pan and heat until the oil is hot. Fry the meat in three batches until well coloured on all sides, adding more oil to the pan if and when needed. Remove the last batch of meat from the pan, then fry the onion, carrots, and garlic until coloured.

Put the meat back in the pan with the vegetables, pour in the stock, and stir well. Bring to the boil. Add salt and pepper and half the thyme, and stir well again. Remove from the heat and divide the beef and vegetables equally among six individual ovenproof dishes (each about 600ml capacity).

Peel the potatoes and slice into 3mm-thick discs. Arrange the discs on top of the beef and vegetables, overlapping them slightly. Brush the potatoes with the melted butter, and sprinkle with salt and pepper and the remaining thyme leaves.

Cover the dishes with lids or foil and bake for 1 hour, then uncover and bake for a further 45 minutes until the meat feels tender when pierced with the tip of a small, sharp knife. Serve hot.

KEY TO PERFECTION

For a richly flavoured hotpot with a good colour and a gravy of substance, the meat needs to be coated in flour and fried until browned at the beginning. Always work in small batches when you're frying meat so you don't overfill the pan – this would make the temperature drop and the meat would stew, not fry.

Put about one-third of the meat in a bowl and sprinkle with one-third of the seasoned flour. Toss with your hands until the meat is evenly coated, then remove and shake off the excess flour. Repeat until all the meat has been coated in this way.

Fry each batch of beef in a single layer in the hot oil until coloured underneath. Resist the urge to turn or prod the meat until it's brown – the less you interfere with it, the sooner it will colour. Once the meat is crisp and browned underneath, turn and repeat on the other sides until the cubes are browned all over. Don't rush this stage or the flour will taste raw in the stew – each batch should take 7–10 minutes.

MUM'S PORK CHOPS

Of all Mum's dishes, this is my favourite, and every time I make it I'm reminded of my childhood. The secrets of its success are the amount of onions used, and the long, slow braising that makes the chops so juicy and tender.

SERVES 4
4 x 150–200g pork loin chops
2 large Spanish onions, peeled
½ bunch of fresh thyme
15 fresh sage leaves
2tsp dried sage
50g cold unsalted butter, diced
Sea salt and freshly milled black pepper

Heat the oven to 160°C fan (180°C/gas 4).

Place the chops in a single layer in a heavy casserole or baking dish. Season well. Cut the onions in half lengthways, then turn them on their cut sides and cut crossways into thin slices. Cover the chops with the onions, separating the slices as you scatter them. Top with the thyme sprigs, fresh and dried sage, and butter. Season well.

Cover the dish with a tight-fitting lid or seal with foil. Bake for about 1½ hours, basting occasionally, until the pork feels tender when pierced with the tip of a sharp knife.

Serve the chops with the onions piled on top, and the buttery juices spooned over and around.

KEY TO PERFECTION

Most pork chops are lean these days, which means they can be tough and chewy – but not if they're baked this way. During the long, slow cooking, the onions give off sweet, natural juices that join forces with the fat from the chops and the butter. This makes a natural sauce, and the meat becomes juicy, tender, and full of flavour.

You need piles of thinly sliced onions and lots of butter to start with. The chops should be completely buried in the onions, so their juices will seep into the chops with the melted butter during cooking.

As the onions soften and the chops gently cook beneath them, juices collect in the bottom of the dish. Two or three times during cooking, remove the lid or foil and tilt the dish so the juices run into one corner. Scoop up the juices with a spoon and drizzle them over the onions and chops.

"Don't worry about the chops overcooking – you need to allow time for the onion juices to be absorbed by the meat. This is the very best way to get tender pork chops."

SAUSAGES WITH ONION GRAVY

Mum used to get sausages and onions ready for when we got home from school. Sometimes she did liver instead of sausages, which we called "leather and onions" because Dad liked everything well cooked and so the liver was chewy. This recipe is my variation on the sausage theme – with a marinade and a touch of alcohol.

SERVES 4
8 large, good-quality pork sausages
2tbsp olive oil
2 red-skinned onions, sliced 5mm thick
3 Spanish onions, sliced 5mm thick
2 garlic cloves, finely chopped
A few sprigs of fresh or dried thyme
200ml red wine or Guinness
2 bay leaves
1 sprig of fresh or dried rosemary
500ml hot Beef Stock (page 11)
A handful of fresh curly parsley, chopped
Sea salt and freshly milled white pepper

FOR THE MARINADE
2tbsp olive oil
A few sprigs of fresh or dried thyme
2 garlic cloves, chopped

Seal the sausages and marinade ingredients in a freezer bag and shake well. Leave in the fridge for a couple of hours, or overnight.

Put a large wok or deep, non-stick frying pan over a low to medium heat. When hot, tip in the contents of the freezer bag and fry for 10–15 minutes until the sausages are golden brown on all sides. Remove the sausages from the pan with a slotted spoon.

Pour the oil into the pan and heat until very hot. Tip in the onions, garlic, and thyme, stir well, and season with a good pinch of salt and a few twists of pepper. Cook over a medium to high heat for about 10 minutes, stirring occasionally, until the onions are caramelized. Meanwhile, boil the wine in a small, heavy saucepan until it has reduced by about one-third.

Tip the wine over the onions and stir in the bay leaves and rosemary. Continue cooking for another 10 minutes, stirring frequently, until the onions are gooey and red.

Add the stock to the onions and mix well, then bring to the boil. Return the sausages to the pan. Turn the heat down to a gentle simmer, cover, and cook for 35 minutes, stirring occasionally.

Throw in the parsley and check for seasoning before serving.

"Lincolnshire sausages are my favourites, so I always like to use them for this dish. They are quite spicy, which is why I season the dish with white pepper rather than black. White pepper is milder."

KEY TO PERFECTION

Using lots of onions gives body to the gravy, while reducing them down brings out their sweetness. This will make the sausages moist and juicy.

For the best-ever gravy, you must start off with a full pan of onions. Don't think you can get away with any less. Using both red and white onions gives extra flavour as well as colour.

Cook the onions with the red wine, stirring occasionally, until they reduce down to a gooey mass. The flavour will become more concentrated as the onions shrink, and the colour will turn a deep burgundy red.

THREE-PEPPER STEAKS

I learnt how to cook steak au poivre when I worked at a French restaurant in Southport with my brother, Brian. We used to flambé the steak at the table – something we also did with steak Diane. Black peppercorns are the classic coating for peppered steak, but they're a little too coarse and hot for me, so I've mellowed them by mixing three different colours of peppercorns together.

SERVES 4
4 x 200g tournedos (thick steaks cut from the centre of the fillet and tied with string)
1tbsp dried green peppercorns
1tsp black peppercorns
1/2tsp white peppercorns
Pinch of sea salt
4tsp Dijon mustard
3tbsp olive oil
75g cold unsalted butter, diced
Pommes Mousseline (page 100), to serve

Take the steaks out of the fridge about half an hour before you want to cook them.

Heat the oven to 190°C fan (210°C/gas 6½).

Coarsely crush the peppercorns and salt in a mortar and pestle. Coat the steaks with the mustard, then with the peppercorns.

Put a large, ovenproof frying pan over a high heat. When hot, pour in the oil and heat until it is hot, then fry the steaks until they are seared all over. Add the butter and let it melt into the hot oil – it calms everything down and turns the fat and juices a nut-brown colour (called *beurre noisette* in French).

Transfer the pan of steaks to the oven. Roast for 4 minutes for rare meat, 7 minutes for medium. Baste the steaks with the juices from the pan halfway through cooking.

Remove the steaks from the oven and allow them to rest in a warm place for about 4 minutes.

Snip the string off the steaks, then cut each steak into four even slices. Arrange on plates, drizzle with the pan juices, and serve the potatoes alongside.

"If you prefer your steaks less peppery, just put peppercorns on the top of each steak, or on the top and bottom. You could also use Sichuan peppercorns instead of the white or green. They are perfumed and spicy rather than hot, and will make a slightly milder-tasting crust."

KEY TO PERFECTION

To get peppered steaks cooked exactly how you like them, the combination of pan-frying and roasting gives best results. If you pan-fry the steaks for the whole cooking time, the peppercorns will scorch and turn bitter.

Brush mustard evenly all over the steaks. This will give the peppercorns a sticky surface to cling to, as well as adding extra flavour to the meat.

Roll the steaks in the crushed peppercorns on a flat surface, and pat them firmly with your hands to make sure they stick evenly. They should cover the sides of each steak, and the top and bottom.

For accurate cooking, sear the steaks in the hot oil for exactly 6 minutes (1 minute on each side and 1 minute each for the top and bottom). The roasting time in the oven then varies, according to how well you like your steak cooked – rare or medium.

SICHUAN CHICKEN

If I want something simple to cook for my boys, Jake and Archie, it's almost always Chinese or chicken. This is one of my favourite stir-fries because I can make it from things we've got in the fridge.

SERVES 4
4 skinless, boneless chicken breasts, cut diagonally across the grain into 5mm-thick strips
5cm piece of fresh root ginger, peeled and very finely chopped
2 garlic cloves, finely chopped
4tbsp vegetable oil
1 carrot, peeled and pared into ribbons with a vegetable peeler
1tsp toasted sesame oil
2 heads of baby pak choi, roots sliced off and leaves separated
5 spring onions, cut into strips on the diagonal
1tsp Sichuan peppercorns, lightly crushed
Sea salt
Fresh coriander leaves, to finish

FOR THE MARINADE
100ml dark soy sauce
100ml mirin (sweet rice wine)
3–4tbsp sake (rice wine)
2tbsp soft brown sugar

Mix all the marinade ingredients together in a bowl, add the chicken strips, and stir to coat. Cover and leave for half an hour, or in the fridge for up to 24 hours.

When you're ready to cook, drain the chicken in a colander set over a bowl. Mix the ginger and garlic into the chicken. Put a wok or large, deep frying pan over a high heat. When hot, pour in the oil and heat until you can see a light haze rising.

Toss in the chicken and leave undisturbed for 2 minutes until coloured underneath, then shake the pan and turn the chicken over. Leave the chicken to sit undisturbed for another 2 minutes until it is coloured on the other side. Remove the chicken with a slotted spoon and set aside.

Add the carrot ribbons to the pan followed by the sesame oil and a pinch of salt. Toss for a minute, then tip in the chicken and its juices, the pak choi, spring onions, and crushed peppercorns. Finish by splashing in some of the marinade and simmering for 3–4 minutes.

Before serving, taste and add more salt or soy sauce if you like, and toss in the coriander leaves.

KEY TO PERFECTION

Chicken breast is very lean, which means it can be bland and dry. Steeping it in a marinade will give it flavour and succulence. The longer you leave it the better, but even as little as half an hour can make a difference.

When you add the chicken to the bowl of marinade, turn the strips so they are evenly coated in the liquid. Then, to make sure the strips get maximum penetration from the liquid and flavourings, stir them as often as you remember during the marinating time.

"You can mix and match the vegetables in this recipe according to what you've got in the salad drawer of your fridge. Spinach, peppers, broccoli, beans, mangetouts, and celery are all good."

CORNED BEEF RÖSTI

We often make these rösti at home. We have them with grilled sausages and bacon, mushrooms, and tomatoes – it makes a great weekend brunch.

MAKES 8
1kg King Edward or Maris Piper potatoes
Fine salt
50g unsalted butter, diced
1 Spanish onion, finely chopped
2 garlic cloves, finely chopped
1 large can (340–375g) corned beef, broken up with a fork
2tbsp brown sauce
1 organic egg, beaten
About 100g natural dried breadcrumbs (from a packet)
About 50g plain white flour, for coating
Olive oil, for frying
Sea salt and freshly milled black pepper
Duck eggs, to serve

Peel the potatoes and grate on the coarse section of a cheese grater. Sprinkle the potatoes lightly with fine salt, then leave to stand for 5–10 minutes. Meanwhile, heat the butter in a frying pan over a high heat until foaming. Add the onion and garlic, season with salt, and cook for 4–5 minutes until soft and golden brown. Remove the pan from the heat.

Now squeeze the moisture out of the potatoes and drop them into a bowl. With your hands, mix in the corned beef, softened onion and garlic, brown sauce, and egg. Add enough breadcrumbs to bind the mixture together. Season well.

Divide the corned beef mix into eight equal portions. Shape into cakes and coat in flour. For a neat edge, press each cake into an 8–10cm pastry ring. Chill for at least 4 hours, or overnight.

Heat the oven to 190°C fan (210°C/gas 6½).

Cover the bottom of a large, non-stick frying pan with olive oil and place over a high heat. When hot, place the rösti in the pan and fry for about 4 minutes on each side until crisp and golden brown. Transfer the rösti to a baking tray and bake for 10–15 minutes, turning halfway. Meanwhile, use the oil in the frying pan to fry as many duck eggs as you like.

Serve the rösti hot, topped with the eggs.

"For Sunday brunch, I get the rösti mix ready the day before and chill it as a log shape wrapped tightly in cling film. It's then really easy to slice into neat rounds just before frying."

KEY TO PERFECTION

For rösti to be crisp and crunchy on the outside, you need to get the potatoes thoroughly dry before shaping and frying the cakes. If the potatoes are wet, water will run out of them into the pan and make the rösti soggy.

Put a sieve over a bowl and line with a cloth. Pick up handfuls of grated potato and squeeze hard to extract as much moisture as possible, then drop the potato into the cloth-lined sieve. Sprinkle with salt and mix well.

After 5–10 minutes, the salt will have drawn moisture out of the potatoes and they will look wet again. Pick them up in the cloth and twist the cloth tightly into a ball shape. Squeeze hard to wring out as much water as possible.

Open the cloth and check the potatoes are dry. If they're not, tip them into a clean, dry cloth and wring again.

ALL IS NOT LOST

If the rösti don't hold their shape when you're frying them, press the whole lot into one big cake. Fry until golden brown underneath, then grill until brown on top. Crack 4 eggs into the centre and bake for 10 minutes until the eggs are set. Serve sprinkled with chopped fresh thyme, sea salt, and olive oil.

BRAISED LAMB SHANKS

I wish I'd known about lamb shanks when I was growing up, because they would have made the perfect Sunday lunch instead of the overcooked roast meat Dad insisted on. This well-done lamb, cooked long and slow, is totally different from overdone roast meat – it's so tender it literally falls off the bone.

SERVES 6
5tbsp olive oil
6 lamb shanks, each weighing about 400g
2 Spanish onions, cut into chunks
2 large carrots, peeled and cut into chunks
1 leek (green part only), cut into chunks
4 celery sticks, strings removed and cut into chunks
4 garlic cloves, peeled and left whole
4 fresh or dried sprigs of rosemary
1/2 bunch of fresh thyme
2tbsp tomato purée
1/2 x 75cl bottle dry white wine
2 litres hot Chicken Stock (page 16)
Sea salt and freshly milled black pepper
Finely chopped fresh rosemary, to finish

Heat the oven to 160°C fan (180°C/gas 4).

Heat the oil in a very large, heavy frying pan (cast iron is good, but non-stick will do). Season the lamb well and sear over a high heat until golden brown underneath before turning and searing on another side. Continue turning and frying until the shanks are nicely coloured all over. Don't rush this stage – it is essential for colour and flavour in the finished dish. The total searing time should be about 20 minutes. Transfer the shanks to a very large, deep casserole.

In the same oil the meat was seared in, fry the vegetables and garlic with the sprigs of rosemary and thyme over a medium heat for about 5 minutes until lightly coloured. Add 1tsp salt and the tomato purée, stir well, and cook for a further 3 minutes. Pour in the wine and reduce by half, then pour in the stock and bring to the boil.

Ladle the liquid and vegetables over the lamb in the casserole. Cover with a cartouche of greaseproof paper, then braise in the oven for 2–2¼ hours. The lamb is done when you can see the meat starting to come away from the bones.

Remove the sprigs of herbs, and check and correct the seasoning of the sauce. Serve in warmed bowls, sprinkled with chopped fresh rosemary.

"For a neat presentation, ask the butcher to French trim the fat off each shank to expose the bone, or do it yourself by scraping the meat and fat from the end of the bone using a sharp knife."

KEY TO PERFECTION

For lamb that is so moist, tender, and soft you can eat it with a spoon, it should be slowly braised in the oven in a covered pan. The secret of success lies in the way it is covered – for this dish, a paper cartouche is more effective than a lid.

Press the cartouche over the surface of the liquid so that it rests directly on it and becomes wet. The paper prevents the meat from drying out, at the same time as letting some steam escape. This allows the liquid to reduce and create a sauce.

Make the cartouche by folding a large rectangle of greaseproof paper in half lengthways, then in half crossways. With the closed corner as the point, fold the paper diagonally in half, then in half again to make a fan shape. Hold the point over the centre of the casserole, cut the paper 5cm larger than the circumference of the pot, and unfold the paper.

VEGETABLES

SPICED AUBERGINES

I got the idea for this dish from *baba ghanoush*, a Middle Eastern dip we serve as a canapé at Pétrus. We spoon it chilled onto toast or French bread croûtons, but, I thought, why not serve it hot as a vegetable? It works amazingly well, and it's lovely with lamb or fish, especially red mullet.

SERVES 4
3 large aubergines
2 large garlic cloves, thinly sliced
2 bay leaves, cut in half
A few sprigs of fresh thyme, snipped into short lengths
2tbsp tomato purée
1tbsp mild curry powder
5tsp ground cumin
4tbsp olive oil
A handful of fresh coriander leaves, chopped
Sea salt and freshly milled black pepper

Heat the oven to 180°C fan (200°C/gas 6).

Cut the aubergines in half lengthways with a sharp knife, then make deep incisions in a small diamond pattern in the flesh of each half without cutting through the skin.

Push the garlic slices, bay leaves, and thyme sprigs into the incisions (the handle of a teaspoon is good for this), then spread the tomato purée over the top and sprinkle with the spices. Season with salt and pepper, and drizzle with a little of the oil.

Sandwich the halves back together, then wrap each aubergine tightly in foil, making sure the whole vegetable is covered. Place in a roasting pan and bake for about 1 hour until soft.

Unwrap the aubergines while they're still hot and separate the halves. Using a spoon, scoop and scrape out the flesh into a sieve suspended over a bowl. Pick out and discard the bay leaves and herb stalks. Leave the aubergine flesh to drain for about half an hour, then tip onto a board and chop roughly.

Place a large, heavy frying pan over a high heat. When hot, pour in the remaining oil and heat it until you can see a haze rising. Add the aubergine flesh and cook for about 5 minutes until the mixture becomes darker in colour and looks quite dry. Stir in the coriander, and check and correct the seasoning if necessary. Serve straightaway.

"To serve as a dip, once the aubergines have cooled, fold in a couple of spoonfuls of natural yogurt and some chopped fresh mint, then chill in the fridge."

KEY TO PERFECTION

The beauty of this dish is the combination of fantastic flavours and silky soft texture.
To get both right, there are two important stages.

Bake the aubergines until they feel
really soft when you squeeze them.
Encasing in foil and cooking for a long
time are essential to allow the flavours
of the herbs, spices, and garlic to
penetrate the deeply scored flesh.

Aubergines give off a lot of liquid,
which will dilute the dish and make it
sloppy if you don't get rid of it. While
the baked flesh is draining, press with
a spoon from time to time, to extract
as much liquid as possible.

SHALLOT TATINS

We serve these topped with melted goat's cheese as part of the vegetarian tasting menu at Pétrus, and as a starter at the Savoy Grill. The contrast between the melt-in-the-mouth sugary shallots and the crisp, buttery pastry makes them totally irresistible.

SERVES 4
375g puff pastry
About 16 even-sized, small shallots
120g caster sugar
80g cold unsalted butter, diced
Sea salt and freshly milled black pepper

You need four 12.5cm non-stick blini pans. Place them on a baking tray and set aside.

On a lightly floured surface, bat the block of pastry with a rolling pin a few times to make it thinner and easier to roll evenly, then cut into quarters and roll out each piece until 3mm thick. Cut out four discs using a pastry cutter or saucer that is 2.5cm bigger than the blini pans. Stack the discs on top of each other with greaseproof paper in between and chill for at least 30 minutes.

Meanwhile, halve the shallots crossways, then trim them to size. Set aside. Heat the oven to 170°C fan (190°C/gas 5). Half fill a roasting pan with cold water and keep by the stove.

Mix the sugar and 3tbsp cold water in a small, heavy saucepan. Put the pan over a medium heat until the sugar has dissolved, then increase the heat to high and cook for 5–10 minutes to an amber-coloured caramel. Don't stir or the sugar will crystallize and go grainy, but occasionally brush down the sides of the pan with a pastry brush dipped in cold water – this will help prevent crystallization.

Whisk the cold butter into the caramel a little at a time (it will foam up and thicken the caramel), then take the pan off the heat and add a few twists of pepper. Pour an equal quantity of caramel into each blini pan – it will harden immediately.

Sprinkle a little salt over the caramel, then pack the shallots in the pans with their widest cut sides facing down. The exact number of shallots you need depends on their size and how tightly you pack them in, but you should get about eight halves in each pan.

Prick each pastry disc all over with a fork. Lay a disc over each pan and tuck well in between the shallots and the edge of the pan. Bake for 20–25 minutes until the pastry is an even golden brown.

Leave the tatins to settle for a few minutes, then invert a small plate over each pan and turn out the tatin onto the plate. Serve hot.

KEY TO PERFECTION

The shallots must all be trimmed to the same size and thickness. If they're not, they will make the pastry uneven and some will be cooked before others.

Cut the roots and tops off the shallots, then cut each shallot crossways in half and peel off the skin. Line them up on a board so you can see which ones are taller, then trim them so they are all the same height.

ALL IS NOT LOST

If the caramel starts to colour too fast and you think it may scorch, quickly dip the base of the pan in the roasting pan of cold water, and hold it there until the cooking has stopped.

"With puff pastry, even rolling equals even rising, and batting it flat before rolling it out is vital for this. Each time you bat the dough, move it round a quarter turn."

MASH

This is my soft, butter-enriched version of mashed potato. It's great with sausages and baked beans, and as a pie topping. When it's enriched with egg yolks, it's good for piping, which is how I use it on my Fish Pie. See pages 50–53.

SERVES 4
1kg King Edward potatoes
A good pinch of fine salt
125g cold unsalted butter, diced
100–200ml hot full-fat milk
¼tsp freshly grated nutmeg
(optional)
Sea salt and freshly milled
white pepper

Peel the potatoes and cut into 4cm pieces. Put the pieces in a saucepan of cold water, add the fine salt, and bring to the boil over a high heat. Lower the heat to medium, cover, and simmer gently (don't boil) for about 20 minutes until soft. Drain well.

Return the potatoes to the pan and dry them out, then remove from the heat and mash until smooth. With a wooden spoon, work the butter into the mash a few pieces at a time, then beat in enough hot milk to give a soft, dropping consistency.

Taste and correct the seasoning if necessary, and add the nutmeg if you like. Serve hot.

KEY TO PERFECTION

For smooth, fluffy mash, it's essential to get the potatoes dry after boiling, and to mash hard before adding the butter and milk.

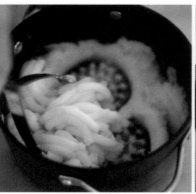

After draining the potatoes, tip them back into the pan and let them steam over a low heat for a few minutes. Shake the pan and toss the potatoes occasionally so they all become dry.

Work hard with the potato masher – it's important to get the potatoes really smooth at this stage, because mashing becomes more difficult once the butter and milk have been added.

Hot milk is essential – it helps smooth out any imperfections in the mash. Pour it in a little at a time and beat hard until it's absorbed before adding more.

POMMES MOUSSELINE

Here's a very special potato dish that is so velvety and rich it's almost like a mousse – hence its name. I learnt how to make it at Le Gavroche in London, and I love it. It's sheer indulgence.

SERVES 6

1kg Ratte potatoes, washed but not peeled
A good pinch of fine salt
300ml full-fat milk
300ml double cream
100g cold unsalted butter, diced
Sea salt and freshly milled black pepper

Put the potatoes in a saucepan and cover with cold water. Add the fine salt, cover, and bring to the boil, then turn the heat down to medium. Simmer gently (don't boil) for about 30 minutes until the potatoes feel soft when gently squeezed. Remove the pan from the heat.

One at a time, take the potatoes out of the water and peel off the skin with a small, sharp knife. As soon as they're all peeled, work them through a food mill.

Tip the puréed potatoes into a clean pan. Bring the milk and cream to boiling point in another pan, then remove from the heat. Using a rubber spatula, beat one-third of the creamy milk into the potatoes over a medium heat, followed by one-third of the butter.

Carry on beating in the milk and butter in two more batches. The potatoes will become shiny and silky smooth. Make sure each batch of milk and butter is fully incorporated before adding the next, and switch to a balloon whisk when the purée gets to the liquid stage.

To serve, taste and correct the seasoning if necessary, then pour the potatoes into a warmed bowl.

"We wear thick rubber gloves to protect our hands when peeling cooked potatoes because the hotter they are, the easier they are to purée. If you let potatoes go cold, they can turn gluey."

KEY TO PERFECTION

For an ultra-smooth purée, you need hot potatoes, hot creamy milk, and a food mill called a mouli. You can use a sieve instead, but it's much harder work, and you need to be careful not to scrape or drag the potatoes across the sieve or they could end up like glue.

Set the mill over a bowl, put a small quantity of hot potatoes in the hopper, and turn the handle to press and work them through. Repeat until all the potatoes are puréed.

The purée should be as smooth as silk after adding all the hot creamy milk and butter, and runny enough to pour from the pan straight into a bowl.

DRESS THE PART

"Put your apron on and clear your working area, then set out your stall by assembling all the ingredients and equipment."

ROAST POTATOES

Dad used to be a fruit and potato merchant in Southport, and potatoes were his passion. His favourites – King Edwards – were the only ones he ever brought home for Mum to cook. I think they're one of the best varieties for roast potatoes, although Maris Piper and Desirée can be used just as well.

SERVES 4
8 large King Edward potatoes, peeled and quartered
Fine salt
100ml vegetable oil
Sea salt, to serve

Put the potatoes in a saucepan, cover with cold water, and add 1½tsp fine salt. Cover and bring to the boil over a high heat, then turn the heat down to medium. Simmer gently (don't boil) for 15 minutes until the potatoes are almost cooked. The tip of a small, sharp knife should go in easily without breaking the potato up.

Heat the oven to 200°C fan (220°C/gas 7).

Drain the potatoes in a colander and shake well, then leave to dry out for a few minutes. Meanwhile, heat the oil in a sturdy roasting pan in the oven until very hot.

Remove the roasting pan from the oven. One by one, carefully place the potatoes in the oil (don't tip them from the colander into the pan or you'll get splashed with hot oil). Season the potatoes with a good pinch of fine salt and turn them in the oil until they're coated, then return the pan to the oven.

Roast the potatoes for 30–40 minutes until crisp and golden. Turn them every 10 minutes, and sprinkle with sea salt about halfway through when they're starting to colour.

Take the potatoes out of the oil with a slotted spoon and drain on kitchen paper. Serve hot, sprinkled with more sea salt.

KEY TO PERFECTION

Golden and crisp on the outside, soft and fluffy inside – these are the perfect roast potatoes. To achieve this result, there are two crucial stages.

Once the potatoes are dry, scratch them all over with a fork. By making the flesh rough on the outside, the hot oil will be able to penetrate into the surface quickly, which will make the potatoes crisp.

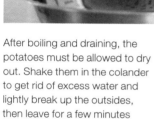

After boiling and draining, the potatoes must be allowed to dry out. Shake them in the colander to get rid of excess water and lightly break up the outsides, then leave for a few minutes for the steam to escape.

ALL IS NOT LOST

If the potatoes aren't getting crisp enough towards the end of cooking, put the pan over a high heat on top of the stove, and toss and turn the potatoes until they crisp up.

SAUTÉ POTATOES

This is the classic French way of sautéing potatoes – with lots of butter. In restaurants they are traditionally served with grilled steak, but they are equally at home with sausages, bacon, and beans.

SERVES 4
16 new Charlotte potatoes, washed but not peeled
1 sprig of fresh or dried thyme
1 garlic clove, lightly crushed
Fine salt
2tbsp olive oil
85–100g cold unsalted butter, diced
Sea salt

Put the potatoes in a saucepan, cover with cold water, and add the thyme, garlic, and a good pinch of fine salt. Cover the pan and bring to the boil over a high heat, then turn the heat down to medium and simmer gently (don't boil) for about 20 minutes.

Check the potatoes by piercing the centre of one with the tip of a small, sharp knife – it should go in easily with just a little resistance (you'll be cooking the potatoes again). Drain and leave to cool.

Cut each potato in half, then slice any large ones into 1cm-thick discs. Heat the oil in a large, non-stick frying pan over a medium-high heat until it gives off a light haze. Place the potatoes in the pan, spread them out, and season with fine salt. Sauté for 3–6 minutes until golden brown underneath. Turn the slices over with a palette knife, season with salt again, and cook for a further 2–3 minutes until the second side is golden brown.

Add the butter and melt it. Shake the pan to coat the potatoes with hot butter, then remove them from the pan with a spatula and drain briefly on kitchen paper. Season with sea salt and serve hot.

KEY TO PERFECTION

Sauté potatoes should be crisp, with a nutty colour and flavour. The way to achieve this is by adding cold butter to the hot oil at the end.

Once the potatoes are crisp on both sides, dot the cubes of butter in between the slices, spacing the butter evenly in the pan.

Shake the pan and watch the butter foam up, then wait a minute or two until it goes nutty brown (*noisette*). Remove from the heat immediately, before it overheats and turns dark.

SPINACH WITH GARLIC AND CREAM

Just as tomatoes go with basil and olive oil, spinach is good with garlic, nutmeg, and cream. For me they are a perfect combination. This dish is a great accompaniment for roast or griddled meat, particularly lamb.

SERVES 2
500g bag baby spinach leaves
200ml double cream
Freshly grated nutmeg
1 fat garlic clove, peeled and cut lengthways into thirds
2tbsp olive oil
Sea salt and freshly milled black pepper

Even though spinach in bags is sold as washed, it's always a good idea to wash it yourself to be sure there's no grit lurking in the leaves. Immerse the leaves in the sink or a large bowl filled with cold water, and swish it about for a minute or so. Drain in a colander, then tip out onto a cloth and gently pat dry. If you notice any stems that are particularly coarse, snap them off.

Put the cream in a heavy saucepan with a few gratings of nutmeg and a pinch of salt. Simmer for 8–10 minutes, stirring often, until you have about 4tbsp left in the bottom of the pan. Remove from the heat.

Spear the garlic onto a fork. Spoon the oil into a wok or a large, deep frying pan and put over a high heat. When the oil is hot, toss in the spinach leaves and season lightly with salt, then stir with the garlic fork until the spinach has wilted.

Tip the contents of the pan into a colander and press the spinach with the garlic fork to get rid of excess water. Tip the spinach back into the pan and reheat, shaking the pan constantly.

Pour the reduced cream over the spinach and stir with the garlic fork until all the leaves are coated with cream. Check the seasoning, then serve the spinach hot.

"Freshly grated nutmeg is always better than ground, but be careful how much you use, as too much can be overpowering."

KEY TO PERFECTION

Although spinach and garlic go really well together, not everyone likes eating pieces of garlic, even when they're finely chopped or crushed. The way to get the flavour without the bits is to use a "garlic fork".

Swish the garlic fork back and forth through the spinach during cooking, shaking the pan at the same time.

Skewer the pieces of garlic firmly onto the tines of a fork, securing them by pushing them down as far as they will go without breaking.

ALL IS NOT LOST

If the dish looks too watery at the end, lift the spinach out with a slotted spoon and drain in a colander set over a bowl. Add the drained liquid to the creamy liquid left in the pan and boil until reduced, then return the spinach to the pan and toss until hot.

BROCCOLI AND BEAN SAUTÉ

Adding crunchy cashews and fresh almonds to broccoli and beans is a really great way of serving these two simple green vegetables. It makes you want to eat them for ever.

SERVES 4

1 large head of broccoli, cut into small florets, with stems trimmed on the diagonal
200g fine French beans, topped but not tailed
3tbsp olive oil, plus extra for drizzling
About 10 unsalted cashew nuts, halved lengthways
About 10 fresh almonds, peeled and halved lengthways
Sea salt

Fill a large bowl half full with cold water and drop in a few handfuls of ice cubes. Set aside.

Plunge the broccoli florets into a large pan of salted boiling water, bring the water back to the boil, and simmer for 1 minute. Drain and refresh in the iced water. Repeat with the beans, then drain both vegetables and dry them on a cloth.

Put the oil in a wok or large, non-stick frying pan and set over a high heat. When you can just see a haze rising, add the cashews and toss until browned. Add the broccoli and sauté for 2 minutes before tossing in the beans. Sauté for another 2 minutes. Remove from the heat and toss in the almonds.

Sprinkle with sea salt, drizzle with olive oil, and serve.

"Fresh almonds are in season in the summer months. They're stronger in flavour than dried. If you can't get them, use dried almonds or sliced canned water chestnuts instead. Dried nuts have a short shelf life, so always buy them from a shop with a fast turnover."

KEY TO PERFECTION

Green vegetables benefit from being blanched in boiling water before sautéing, so they will cook quickly in the hot oil and not get too brown. The secret of keeping their bright colour is to "refresh" them in iced water immediately after blanching. This stops the cooking straightaway and sets the colour.

Plunge the hot, drained vegetables into the bowl of iced water. Leave until they are cold, then drain. The colour will stay bright green.

ONE-POT ROAST VEGETABLES

I created this dish when we had friends coming round for Sunday lunch. I didn't want to spend hours at the stove while they were there, so before they arrived I put the joint of meat in the oven in one roasting pan and the vegetables in another. This left me with very little cooking to do until just before serving time.

SERVES 4
150ml vegetable oil
3 parsnips, cut into 5cm pieces
1 celeriac, weighing about 400g, peeled and cut into 5cm pieces
500g baby new potatoes, preferably Jersey Royals, washed and left whole, or halved if large
4 carrots, peeled and cut into 5cm pieces on the diagonal
2–3 celery sticks, strings removed and cut into 5cm pieces on the diagonal
12 cipolline onions, quartered lengthways
1 bulb garlic, broken open without peeling the cloves
1–2 unwaxed lemons, cut lengthways into wedges
5 sprigs of fresh rosemary
10 sprigs of fresh thyme
4 bay leaves
Sea salt and freshly milled black pepper

Heat the oven to 200°C fan (220°C/gas 7).

Put the oil in a large, heavy roasting pan and heat in the oven for about 5 minutes until a light haze rises off the oil. Carefully add all the vegetables, the garlic, lemon wedges, and herbs to the hot oil, season, and stir well to mix.

Return the pan to the oven and roast for 50 minutes to 1 hour, stirring every 20 minutes, until the vegetables are tender and tinged with brown. Serve straightaway.

"Cipolline are small, flat Italian onions. I particularly like their sweet flavour with the other vegetables in this dish, but you can use shallots instead."

KEY TO PERFECTION

To be sure all the different vegetables cook in the same amount of time, they must be cut into similar-sized pieces. Some are easier to deal with than others.

Celeriac is unwieldy to prepare because it's so hard and knobbly, but it's well worth including for its nutty flavour. After peeling it thickly and trimming off the ends, cut it vertically into quarters. Now you'll find it easy to cut the quarters into neat pieces.

Parsnips need special attention because they often have tough, woody cores, especially if they are large or old. Before cutting them into pieces, quarter them lengthways and cut off the hard ridge running down the inside edge of each piece.

Although the vegetables start off completely different in shape and size, when cut into uniform shapes they'll become tender at the same time.

BITTERSWEET CHICORY SALAD

Years ago I had a salad like this at Le Caprice, and I've never forgotten it. I loved the taste of the bitter chicory tossed in a mustard dressing sweetened with honey. Here I've used a sharp, crisp apple instead of honey, which gives the salad a lovely sweet and sour flavour.

SERVES 4
1 head of red chicory
1 head of white chicory
1 head of curly endive (frisée)
5 sprigs of fresh coriander
2 Granny Smith apples
4tbsp Vinaigrette Dressing (below)

Separate the chicory leaves and cut them lengthways in half if they are large. Separate the curly endive leaves; use only the lightest leaves from the centre. Pick the leaves off the coriander stalks. Rinse all the leaves in cold water, drain them in a colander, and dry well by shaking in a cloth.

Peel, quarter, and core the apples. Cut the quarters into thin slices and then into matchsticks.

Mix the leaves and apples together in a large bowl.

Pour the dressing over the salad in the bowl and toss gently with your hands until all the leaves are coated. Serve straightaway.

VINAIGRETTE DRESSING

MAKES ABOUT 300ML
1 heaped tbsp Dijon mustard
About 4tbsp white wine vinegar
250ml extra-virgin olive oil
Sea salt and freshly milled
black pepper

Whisk the mustard with a good pinch each of salt and pepper. Whisk in 2tbsp vinegar, then gradually whisk in the oil. Taste and add more vinegar and seasoning if you like. Keep in a screw-top jar in the fridge. Before use, shake well to emulsify the dressing again, then taste and correct the seasoning if necessary.

KEY TO PERFECTION

Fresh salad leaves need a good dressing to bring out their flavour. Vinaigrette is the classic oil and vinegar combination, and the ratio of one to another is as important as the way they are mixed. I use five parts oil to one part vinegar, which is rather more oil than in most recipes, but to me it's the perfect balance – any more vinegar and it would kill off the taste of the leaves.

After mixing the mustard and seasonings to make a thick base, the oil will quickly emulsify when you whisk it in. Add it slowly in a thin, steady stream, whisking vigorously.

When all the oil has been incorporated, the dressing will be beautifully creamy and thick.

Use your hands to gently toss the salad leaves and dressing together. This way you can be sure all the leaves are lightly and evenly coated, and the leaves will not be bruised.

GREEN SALAD WITH HERBS

Try to get as much variety as possible in your leafy salads, both for looks and for flavour. There are no hard-and-fast rules. Simply buy what's freshest and best on the day. That's the beauty of making your own salad – it's different every time.

SERVES 4–6
50g wild baby rocket leaves
20g Lollo Rosso leaves
20g ruby chard leaves
1 head of curly endive (frisée), light green leaves only
1 bunch of watercress, leaves only
5tbsp pea shoots (optional)
5tbsp fresh chervil leaves
5tbsp fresh coriander leaves
2tbsp fresh tarragon leaves
About 24 fresh basil leaves, torn
2 punnets of mustard and cress, snipped with scissors
4–5tbsp Vinaigrette Dressing (page 114)
Sea salt and freshly milled black pepper

Rinse, drain, and dry all the salad and herb leaves. Put them in a large bowl.

Add the dressing and toss gently with your hands until all the leaves are evenly coated with dressing.

Pile the salad in individual bowls and serve straightaway.

KEY TO PERFECTION

The leaves must be thoroughly dry. If they are wet, the dressing won't cling to them and the salad will be watery and insipid.

After rinsing the leaves under the cold tap, shake and turn them in a colander to remove excess water.

Tip the leaves out of the colander, then line the colander with a cloth. Drop in a handful of leaves and enclose loosely in the cloth. Shake gently to get the leaves as dry as possible, then tip them out and repeat with the remainder.

"Salad leaves are delicate and should be handled with care.
Don't use a salad spinner for drying because it will bruise them."

TOMATO SALAD

To me there is nothing more refreshing than a well-chilled tomato salad, at any time of year. I sometimes cut the tomatoes into smaller pieces and serve them as a salsa with griddled chicken or steak.

SERVES 4
500–600g ripe tomatoes, hulls removed
1 branch of ripe cherry tomatoes on the vine (about 8 tomatoes)
3–4 shallots, finely sliced into rings
A few sprigs each of fresh basil and coriander
A handful of wild baby rocket leaves
4tbsp Vinaigrette Dressing (page 114)
Sea salt and freshly milled black pepper

Blanch, refresh, and drain the ordinary tomatoes (not the cherry tomatoes). Peel and quarter them, then put them in a bowl.

Snip the cherry tomatoes off the vine into the bowl and add the shallots. Pick the basil and coriander leaves off the stalks and drop into the bowl. Add the rocket, then drizzle over the dressing and toss gently to mix. Cover and chill for a couple of hours.

Before serving, taste and correct the seasoning if necessary.

"If the tomatoes are peeled, the dressing can draw out their juices as if making them bleed, and this accentuates their flavour."

KEY TO PERFECTION

If you are lucky enough to get homegrown or Mediterranean tomatoes in the summer you can eat them as they are. At other times of the year, tomato skins can be tough, and will spoil an otherwise good tomato salad, so it is best to remove them.

With a sharp knife, make a shallow, cross-shaped incision in the rounded end of each tomato. This will help loosen the skin during blanching.

Blanch the tomatoes by immersing them in a pan of boiling water for 10–30 seconds until you see the skins start to split.

Lift the tomatoes out of the hot water with a slotted spoon as soon as the skins split, then plunge immediately into iced water. Leave to cool for 5 minutes, then remove and drain on a cloth or kitchen paper.

Peel off the skins with a small, sharp knife – they will come away easily.

SWEET PEPPER SALAD

This salad is great served warm with grilled fish or burgers, and is equally good cold with cheese. At Pétrus we also serve it at room temperature as a relish, with fish like John Dory and red mullet.

SERVES 4
100ml olive oil
4 red peppers
4 yellow peppers
1 small bunch of fresh thyme
2 red-skinned onions, thinly sliced
4 garlic cloves, thinly sliced
A handful of fresh basil leaves, thinly sliced
A handful of fresh marjoram leaves
Sea salt and freshly milled black pepper

Heat the oven to 200°C fan (220°C/gas 7).

Put 3tbsp of the oil in a heavy roasting pan and place over a high heat. When hot, add the whole peppers, a few thyme sprigs, and salt and pepper. Fry for about 10 minutes until the peppers are tinged brown on all sides. Transfer the pan to the oven and roast the peppers for 10 minutes until softened. Immediately put the peppers in a large bowl and cover tightly with cling film. Leave to cool.

Peel the skin off the peppers. Cut each pepper in half lengthways and cut off the stalk end, then scrape out the seeds and ribs from inside. Slice the flesh lengthways into 5mm-wide strips. Reserve the pepper juices.

Heat 2tbsp oil in a frying pan over a medium heat until hot. Add the onions with the garlic and the remaining thyme and sauté for a few minutes. Season with salt, then cook until the onions are lightly coloured and softening. Remove the thyme. Add the peppers and seasoning and cook for a further 2 minutes. Transfer to a bowl, add the reserved pepper juices, and leave to cool a little.

To serve, stir the basil and marjoram through the peppers, drizzle with the remaining oil, and sprinkle with sea salt.

"To keep these peppers as a relish, add a few spoonfuls of wine vinegar and store in a Kilner or other tightly sealed jar in the fridge."

KEY TO PERFECTION

Pepper skin is tough, so it's best to peel peppers for a salad. Many recipes suggest charring the skin over a gas flame to loosen it, but this can make the peppers taste bitter. A combination of frying and roasting gives a sweeter result.

When frying the peppers, let them sit undisturbed until the skin colours and starts to blister underneath before turning them and browning the next side.

Cool the fried and roasted peppers in a bowl sealed with cling film. The steam inside will loosen the skins and make the peppers juicy. Wait until they are cold before removing the film.

Peel off the skin with a small knife – it will come away easily. Have a bowl of warm water to hand, so you can keep dipping the knife in to keep it clean.

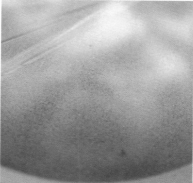
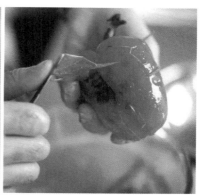

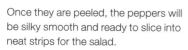

Once they are peeled, the peppers will be silky smooth and ready to slice into neat strips for the salad.

PASTA, PULSES & GRAINS

BAKED PENNE WITH BOLOGNESE

My sister, Tracy, always made the bolognese sauce, and ever since leaving home I've noticed that whatever house or flat I've lived in there's been someone who could make a good bolognese. This baked version is a great dish to feed a crowd, because it can be prepared ahead and cooked when you need it.

SERVES 6
2tsp fine salt
500g dried penne rigate
(or plain penne if you prefer)
Olive oil
500g Taleggio cheese,
thinly sliced
2tbsp chopped fresh flat-leaf
parsley, to finish

FOR THE BOLOGNESE SAUCE
3tbsp olive oil
50g unsalted butter
1 large Spanish onion,
finely chopped
4 celery sticks, strings
removed and finely chopped
2 carrots, peeled and
finely chopped
3 garlic cloves, finely chopped
4 sprigs of fresh thyme
4 sprigs of fresh marjoram
2 bay leaves
500g lean minced beef
2tbsp tomato purée
10 ripe plum tomatoes,
peeled (page 119), deseeded,
and chopped, or 400g can
chopped tomatoes
Sea salt and freshly milled
black pepper

First make the bolognese sauce. Heat the oil and butter in a large, heavy pan over a medium heat. Add the vegetables, garlic, and herbs, and cook until the vegetables are light golden brown. Add the minced beef and cook until it starts to colour, stirring to break up any lumps. Season and stir in the tomato purée. Cook for a further 5 minutes, then stir in the tomatoes and 200ml water. Cover and cook over a low heat for 1 hour, stirring occasionally.

Bring a large pan of water to a rapid boil over a high heat. Add the salt, then the pasta and stir well. Cover the pan and bring the water back to the boil, then take the lid off and turn the heat down slightly. Boil for 10–12 minutes, or according to pack instructions, stirring frequently, until the pasta is al dente (tender, but still with a little bite).

Heat the oven to 170°C fan (190°C/gas 5).

Drain the pasta well in a colander and tip into a very large bowl. Pour the sauce into the bowl and mix well, moistening with a splash of olive oil. Taste for seasoning. Transfer to a large baking dish and lay the slices of Taleggio on top, overlapping them slightly. Bake for 30 minutes until the cheese is golden brown and bubbling. Serve hot, sprinkled with chopped parsley and black pepper.

KEY TO PERFECTION

You can cook pasta following the directions on the pack, but there are a couple of things they may not tell you that can make a big difference to the success of the finished dish – adding the pasta to water that is boiling rapidly and keeping it on the move.

The water should be at a rolling boil when the pasta goes in, so it will start cooking straightaway and you can time it accurately. To make sure of this, bring the water to the boil and throw in the salt, then watch the water surge. This is your cue to put in the pasta.

After the water has returned to the boil, remove the lid, then stir the pasta frequently during cooking to prevent the pieces clumping together.

LINGUINE WITH PESTO

When I was staying in a holiday cottage in Devon with my family, we had a trip out to a farmer's market one morning and bought some locally grown basil and garlic. I used these to quickly knock up some pesto sauce and pasta for lunch. Pesto is fantastic if it's freshly made and eaten straightaway. The colour and flavour are incredibly intense, totally different from the pesto you buy in the shops.

SERVES 4–6
2tsp fine salt
500g dried linguine
Extra-virgin olive oil, for drizzling
Grated fresh Parmesan cheese, to serve

FOR THE PESTO
Leaves of 1 large bunch of fresh basil, weighing about 65g
50g pine nuts, toasted
1 garlic clove, finely chopped
40g fresh Parmesan cheese, grated
200ml extra-virgin olive oil
Sea salt and freshly milled black pepper

Bring a large pan of water to a rapid boil over a high heat. Add the fine salt, immediately coil the pasta into the water, and cover the pan. Bring the water back to the boil, then take the lid off the pan and turn the heat down slightly. Boil for 10–12 minutes, or according to pack instructions, stirring frequently, until the pasta is al dente (tender, but still with a little bite).

Make the pesto while the pasta is cooking. Pulse the basil leaves with the pine nuts, garlic, Parmesan, and seasoning in the blender a few times, then pulse in the oil, drizzling it through the hole in the lid. Stop occasionally to scrape down the sides.

Drain the pasta well in a colander and tip into a large bowl. Drizzle with a splash of olive oil and toss to keep the strands separate, then add the pesto and toss again until the pasta is evenly coated.

Divide among warmed bowls, drizzle with olive oil, and top with grated Parmesan. Serve straightaway.

KEY TO PERFECTION

Basil is one of the most delicate of herbs. It bruises easily, and quickly loses aroma and flavour once it's cut, so for the brightest colour and freshest taste, the less it's chopped the better. This is why pesto should be made quickly, have a rough and ready texture, and be eaten as soon as possible after it's made.

Pick the basil leaves off their stems and drop them into the blender. Add the remaining pesto ingredients, except the oil, then pulse a few times – just until roughly chopped.

Work the oil into the pesto with the blender on pulse. Check how it's doing after every pulse or two, and stop while it's still chunky. Don't grind it to a purée – you should see flecks of pine nuts in amongst the basil.

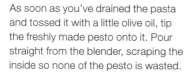

As soon as you've drained the pasta and tossed it with a little olive oil, tip the freshly made pesto onto it. Pour straight from the blender, scraping the inside so none of the pesto is wasted.

TAGLIATELLE WITH CRAB

It's hard to capture the delicate flavour of crab, which is why I like to mix some brown meat in with the white – brown meat has a deeper crab flavour than white. Don't be tempted to add more brown meat than the quantity I suggest or it will be overpowering.

SERVES 4

½ quantity fresh Pasta Dough (opposite)
2tbsp olive oil, plus extra for drizzling
2 shallots, very finely chopped
2 garlic cloves, finely sliced
2 fat fresh red chillies, deseeded and very finely chopped
70g fresh brown crab meat, finely chopped
300g fresh white crab meat, picked over to remove all shell
5–6tbsp very finely chopped fresh flat-leaf parsley
2tsp fine salt
Sea salt and freshly milled black pepper

Divide the pasta dough in half. On a floured surface, roll out each piece into a strip that is roughly the same width as your pasta machine. Sprinkle the strips with flour and roll each one through the machine until the dough is very smooth, thin, and even. Machines vary, but most require the dough to be rolled through many times, working down from the highest notch to the lowest with each rolling, sprinkling with flour in between. When the strips get too long to handle, cut them into two short lengths before the next rolling. If the pasta looks too coarse at the end, fold the strips in four and roll them through again, from the highest notch down to the lowest.

Cut the pasta into tagliatelle with the machine, then hang the ribbons on a floured, clean broom handle.

Heat the oil in a non-stick frying pan over a low to medium heat and fry the shallots, garlic, and chillies with salt and pepper until soft. Add the brown crab meat and stir to mix, then gently fold in the white crab meat and parsley. Remove from the heat and keep warm.

Bring a large pan of water to a rapid boil over a high heat. Add the fine salt, then immediately drop in the pasta, give it a quick stir, and cover the pan. Bring the water back to the boil. Take the lid off the pan and turn the heat down a little. Boil the tagliatelle for 2–3 minutes, stirring occasionally, until it is tender.

Drain the tagliatelle well in a colander and tip into a large bowl. Drizzle with olive oil and toss gently to coat the strands, then tip in the crab mixture and toss gently again until all the pasta is evenly coated. Serve straightaway, with more olive oil for drizzling if you like.

"I always make more pasta dough than I need because I find it works better with a large quantity of flour and eggs. The leftover dough will keep in the fridge for a couple of days."

PASTA DOUGH

MAKES ABOUT 900G
550g "00" pasta flour
1tsp fine salt
4 large organic eggs
6 large organic egg yolks
2tbsp olive oil

Tip the flour and salt into a food processor fitted with the metal chopping blade. Beat the eggs and egg yolks together in a jug, then pour about one-third into the machine and pulse to mix. With the machine running, add the oil and more of the eggs through the funnel. You'll need only enough egg to make the mixture look crumbly. Don't overwork it. Turn out onto a floured surface and knead until smooth. Wrap in cling film and refrigerate for at least 1 hour before using.

KEY TO PERFECTION

Making your own pasta dough is easy. This recipe has a large quantity of eggs and egg yolks, which produces a very rich and silky pasta.

After doing the squeeze test, don't worry when the mix turns out of the machine like a messy crumble. It will soon come together when you start kneading.

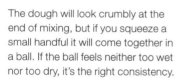

The dough will look crumbly at the end of mixing, but if you squeeze a small handful it will come together in a ball. If the ball feels neither too wet nor too dry, it's the right consistency.

To knead the dough, push it away from you with the heel of your hand, then roll it back on itself towards you to fold it in half, and push it away again. The dough is kneaded to stretch the gluten so the pasta will be light and silky.

Stop kneading when the dough is smooth and matt, not shiny. Form into a ball, wrap in cling film, and let it relax in the fridge for at least an hour (6 hours or overnight is best). Don't skip this stage or the dough will be too springy to roll.

EGG FRIED RICE

A Chinese restaurant was my first taste of foreign cuisine. I usually played safe and ordered egg fried rice, because it looked the most familiar dish on the menu. Even though I gradually got braver and started eating more adventurous things, it's still one of my favourites.

SERVES 4
500g long-grain rice
Pinch of fine salt
2tbsp vegetable oil
4 large organic eggs, beaten
Soy sauce, to taste

Wash, drain, and rinse the rice until the water is clear.

Fill a large pan with water, bring to the boil, and add the salt. The large amount of water is important – it helps to dilute the starch, like the initial rinsing, and to keep the grains of rice separate.

Add the rice to the water, stir, and boil uncovered over a high heat for 10–12 minutes until the rice is tender. Drain in a sieve, rinse, and pat dry, then leave to dry out and cool for about half an hour.

Place a non-stick wok or large, deep frying pan over a high heat. When hot, add the oil and heat until you can see a light haze rising. Pour in the eggs, and cook and stir until lightly scrambled.

Tip in the rice. Stir and toss the rice and eggs together until the rice is piping hot and the eggs are evenly mixed through, then sprinkle with soy sauce to taste. Toss to mix and serve straightaway.

"If you add a lot of salt to the water when boiling rice it can rupture the grains and make them stick together. For this reason, only add the smallest amount of salt – just enough to bring out the flavour."

KEY TO PERFECTION

Rice tends to stick when it's being fried, even in a non-stick pan. To prevent this happening, you need to get rid of as much starch as possible from the rice before you start frying, and the rice must be cold and dry.

Before boiling the rice, put it in a large bowl and fill two-thirds full with cold water, then swish it around with your fingers to release the starch. The water will turn cloudy and milky white. Tip the rice into a large sieve and let the water drain through, then rinse the rice under the cold tap.

Put the rice back in the rinsed-out bowl, fill with fresh cold water as before, and swish again. This time the water will be less cloudy. Drain and rinse the rice, and repeat until the water remains clear.

When the rice has boiled until tender, drain it in a large sieve. Hold under the cold tap to stop the cooking, shaking the sieve to make sure every grain of rice gets rinsed. The longer you rinse the better, as this will wash off the last of the starch. Now tip the rice onto a large plate or tray, spread it out, and pat off the excess moisture with a clean cloth or kitchen paper.

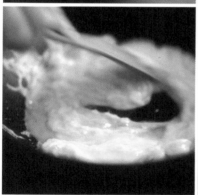

Cooking the eggs first will also help to prevent the rice from sticking to the pan. Add the beaten eggs to the hot oil and tilt the pan from side to side so the eggs cover the bottom, then quickly stir with a wooden spatula for a couple of minutes until the eggs are lightly scrambled.

RISOTTO

This is a calming, effortless dish. I just love to stand stirring at the stove, at one with my risotto – and a glass of chilled dry white wine. You have to open a bottle for cooking after all.

SERVES 4
About 1.3 litres hot Chicken
Stock (page 16)
1 sprig of fresh thyme
3tbsp olive oil
2 shallots, finely chopped
1 small garlic clove,
finely chopped
500g Carnaroli or Vialone
Nano rice
A good splash of dry
white wine
Sea salt and freshly milled
black pepper

TO FINISH
About 50g fresh Parmesan
cheese (30g grated and
20g shaved), plus more
to taste
50g cold unsalted butter, diced
50g mascarpone

Put the stock and thyme in a pan and bring to the boil, then leave at a gentle simmer on the stove.

Heat the oil in a large, deep heavy pan over a medium heat. Add the shallots and garlic, and cook for a few minutes without colouring until they start to soften.

Tip in the rice, and stir and cook for a few minutes until it becomes shiny and translucent. Now listen for a popping sound – this is the sign that the rice is ready for the liquid to be added. Splash in the wine and let it reduce to nothing, stirring constantly.

Add a ladleful of the hot stock, season, and stir. Simmer, stirring, until you can no longer see the stock, then add the rest of the stock a ladleful at a time, stirring constantly until each has been absorbed before adding the next. The total cooking time for the risotto should be 15–20 minutes.

To check if the risotto is done, shake the pan and toss the rice. If it's loose enough to find its own way round the pan, it's ready. If not, add a little more stock and continue to cook until you are happy with the consistency. Another way to check is to taste a few grains of rice. If there's a chalky crunch on the outside, cook for a few more minutes.

To finish, stir in 30g grated Parmesan, then the butter two pieces at a time, and finally the mascarpone. Taste for seasoning and add more grated Parmesan if you like. Serve in wide, shallow bowls topped with the shaved Parmesan.

"Mascarpone isn't a classic ingredient in risotto, and it's not essential to include it in this recipe, but it does make the rice very rich and creamy, which is how I like it."

KEY TO PERFECTION

A perfectly cooked risotto should be creamy in consistency, not sloppy or mushy, and the grains of rice should retain some bite. Get the stock hot and all the other ingredients prepared in advance, and stand over the pan for the whole time the risotto is cooking. Don't walk away from it, not even for a minute.

At the beginning, get the flavour base of shallots and garlic nice and soft before shooting the rice into the pan all in one go. Stir immediately to coat the rice in the oil and shallots.

After cooking the rice until it is translucent, and reducing the wine until it's all gone, you will be able to draw a line through the rice with the spatula. Now you can start adding the hot chicken stock.

The stock must be added in small batches – wait until each batch is absorbed before adding the next – while stirring constantly. Stirring keeps the rice active and moving, which releases the starch from the grains to make the risotto creamy.

ALL IS NOT LOST

If you've overcooked the rice (or you've got some risotto left over), chill it in the fridge until firm, then shape into balls or flat cakes. Coat in flour, then in beaten egg and breadcrumbs, and fry in olive oil until golden and crisp.

BE PREPARED

"Before starting to cook, weigh and measure ingredients and complete any preparation steps like peeling, slicing, and chopping."

COUSCOUS WITH CANDIED LEMON

It was when I worked in New York with Daniel Boulud that I discovered how to make candied lemons. Later, when Pétrus opened in London, I used the lemons to garnish duck. Now I prefer to mix them into the couscous we serve with duck. They really add something special.

SERVES 4
200g fine couscous
250ml hot Chicken Stock
(page 16)
75g raisins
50–75g shelled pistachio nuts,
toasted and roughly chopped
A handful of fresh coriander
leaves, chopped
A splash of Vinaigrette
Dressing (page 114)

FOR THE CANDIED LEMON
150g caster sugar
1 small lemon, very thinly
sliced and pips removed

First candy the lemon. Mix the sugar with 150ml cold water in a heavy saucepan and bring to the boil over a medium heat. Add the lemon slices. Reduce the heat so the liquid is barely simmering and cook for 40 minutes to 1 hour until the slices are soft and syrupy.

Meanwhile, put the couscous in a large bowl and whisk in the stock. Cover tightly with cling film and leave in a warm place for at least 30 minutes, whisking several times. Put the raisins in a small bowl, cover with warm water, and leave to soak.

Remove the lemon slices from the syrup. When cool enough to handle, chop into small pieces. Drain the raisins and chop roughly.

Fluff up the couscous, add about one-third of the chopped lemon with the raisins and pistachios, and mix well. Serve at cool room temperature, or warm through in a bowl set over a pan of simmering water for a few minutes. Before serving, stir in the coriander and dressing, then check the seasoning and add more lemon if you like.

KEY TO PERFECTION

Couscous should be light and fluffy, with individual grains that have a nutty texture when you bite into them. There should be no lumps or clumps of couscous stuck together.

As you pour in the hot stock, whisk constantly to separate the couscous grains. They will then be free to absorb the stock during standing.

At the end of soaking, the couscous will have increased in volume and the grains will be swollen and plump. Stroke through them with a fork and separate any clumps with your fingers.

CHILLI BEANS

I devised this dish when I was working at The Point in upstate New York. Some of the guests didn't want dinner in the restaurant because they wanted to watch football on television – it was Sunday evening and the NFL was on. I made this off the top of my head, and they ate it with nachos, bread, and beer while they watched the game in the manager's flat. It was a great success.

SERVES 4–6
50g dried red kidney beans, soaked in cold water overnight and drained
50g dried green adzuki beans, soaked in cold water for a few hours and drained
30g Puy lentils
5tbsp olive oil
1 Spanish onion, finely chopped
2 red peppers, finely chopped
2 hot red chillies, deseeded and finely chopped
2 garlic cloves, finely chopped
2tsp chilli powder (medium or hot, to taste)
300g ripe tomatoes, peeled (page 119), deseeded, and chopped, or 400g can chopped tomatoes
500ml tomato juice
Leaves of 1 bunch of fresh coriander, roughly chopped
Sea salt and freshly milled black pepper

Blanch, drain, and rinse the kidney beans, then return them to the rinsed-out pan and cover generously with fresh cold water. Bring to the boil over a high heat again, and boil rapidly without the lid for 10 minutes. Half cover the pan, turn down the heat, and simmer the beans for 30–45 minutes until tender.

Meanwhile, blanch the adzuki beans and lentils as for the kidney beans, using a separate pan for each. Drain and rinse, then bring both to the boil in separate pans of water. Half cover the pans and simmer until tender, allowing 12–15 minutes for the adzuki beans, 20–25 minutes for the lentils. Drain the kidney and adzuki beans and the lentils, and set aside.

Heat the olive oil in a heavy pan over a medium heat and add the onion, red peppers, chillies, and garlic. Sprinkle in the chilli powder and a pinch of salt. Cook for 5 minutes until the vegetables are softened, stirring occasionally. Add the tomatoes followed by the beans, lentils, and tomato juice, and stir well to mix. Cover and simmer over a low heat for 45 minutes to 1 hour, stirring occasionally, until the sauce has thickened.

Stir some of the coriander into the beans and add seasoning to taste. Serve with the remaining coriander sprinkled on top.

"If you are short of time, use canned beans and lentils – you can use any type of beans you like."

KEY TO PERFECTION

To help make red kidney beans easier to digest by reducing their gassy effect, and to get rid of any toxins, blanch and boil them rapidly before leaving them to cook.

At the start of cooking, rapidly boil the beans for 10 minutes. This will destroy any toxins that red kidney beans may contain. With a ladle, scoop off the scum as it rises to the surface during this time – this will keep the water clear.

To blanch the beans, put them in a saucepan of cold water and bring to the boil over a high heat. Drain immediately in a colander, hold the colander under the cold tap, and rinse the beans thoroughly to wash off all the scum.

ALL IS NOT LOST

If the chilli beans get overcooked and turn mushy, just strain off the excess liquid by tipping the beans into a sieve, then purée them in a blender or food processor. Chill and serve as a dip, topped with a few whole beans, some chopped coriander, and a sprinkling of paprika and olive oil.

LENTILS WITH HERBS

Don't push pulses to the back of the cupboard – they deserve better treatment. When you make an effort and add interesting things to them, you'll be amazed how good they are – and they're good for you too. It's time they lost their boring image.

SERVES 4
150g Puy lentils
500ml Vegetable Nage (page 22)
2 small carrots, peeled and halved lengthways
1 onion, cut lengthways into chunks
1 small leek, cut into chunks
1 celery stick, strings removed and cut crossways in half
1 sprig of fresh thyme

FOR THE SECOND STAGE
3 shallots, very finely chopped
1/2 celery stick, strings removed and very finely chopped
1/2 carrot, peeled and very finely chopped
50–100g cold unsalted butter, diced
About 3tbsp finely chopped fresh herbs (parsley, chervil, and chives)
Sea salt and freshly milled black pepper

Rinse the lentils in a sieve under the cold tap, tip into a saucepan, and cover generously with cold water. Bring to the boil, then drain in the sieve and rinse well again.

Tip the lentils into the rinsed-out pan and pour in half the nage and 250ml cold water. Add the vegetables and thyme. Stir, then cover closely with a piece of greaseproof paper and bring to the boil. Turn the heat down and simmer gently for 5–8 minutes until the lentils are half cooked. Drain in a sieve and remove the vegetables and thyme.

For the second stage, return the lentils to the rinsed-out pan and pour in the remaining nage. Add the finely chopped shallots, celery, and carrot, and bring to the boil over a medium to high heat. Reduce the heat and simmer gently, uncovered, for about 10 minutes until there is half as much liquid as lentils.

Add as much butter as you like, a little at a time, stirring until it is all incorporated – the end result should be a shiny emulsion. Stir in the chopped herbs, season, and serve straightaway.

KEY TO PERFECTION

Unlike dried beans, lentils don't need soaking and they cook very quickly, but they should be blanched before they're cooked with other ingredients. If you don't do this, the finished dish will be murky and grey.

Blanch the lentils by putting them in a pan of cold water and bringing them to the boil. Drain in a sieve and rinse well under the cold tap to wash away all the discoloured water.

When the lentils have been blanched, they will readily absorb the flavours of the chunky vegetables and fresh thyme.

EGGS

SCRAMBLED EGGS

We often have scrambled eggs at home on Saturday mornings, either for breakfast or brunch, depending on what time we get out of bed. Sometimes I make them, sometimes my wife does – it's whoever goes downstairs first. The boys like scrambled eggs on buttered crumpets rather than toast.

SERVES 2
6 large organic eggs
2tbsp double cream
A splash of milk
50g unsalted butter, diced
Sea salt and freshly milled
black pepper

TO SERVE
Buttered toasted crumpets
Snipped fresh chives

Lightly whisk the eggs with the cream and milk in a bowl, and season with a little salt.

Put a large, non-stick frying pan over a low heat until hot. Add the butter and heat until foaming, then pour in the eggs and move them slowly around the bottom and side of the pan. Keep them moving like this for 2–3 minutes until the eggs look soft and creamy.

Immediately remove the pan from the heat and spoon the eggs onto the hot buttered crumpets. Sprinkle with snipped chives and black pepper, and serve straightaway.

KEY TO PERFECTION

For soft and creamy scrambled eggs, you need to know exactly when to start cooking – and when to stop. Even over a low heat, the eggs will be done sooner than you think.

 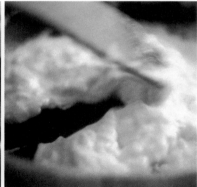

While the eggs are slowly scrambling, keep them on the move. Scrape them constantly off the bottom and side of the pan with a flat wooden spatula (this will get into the edge of the pan better than a spoon), and be ready to whip the pan off the heat when the first large "curds" appear. The eggs will continue to cook in their own heat after they've been taken off the stove, so it's vital to stop cooking at this point or they'll become rubbery and watery.

Get the butter hot and foaming before you pour in the eggs. The heat of the butter will then start the eggs cooking the second they run over the bottom of the pan.

FRIED EGGS BANJO

I got the name "banjo" from my granddad. It's an old Army term for a fried egg sandwich made with stale bread, margarine, and ketchup or brown sauce. This is my version, using slightly better ingredients!

SERVES 2
1 small flat loaf of country bread (eg petit parisienne)
Olive oil, for drizzling
50g cold unsalted butter, cut into 8 cubes
4 large organic eggs
Tomato ketchup
Sea salt and freshly milled black pepper

Cut the loaf in half through the middle, as if making a large sandwich. Heat a dry griddle pan until it is very hot. Drizzle olive oil over the cut sides of the loaf and rub it in, then chargrill the halves cut-side down on the hot griddle pan.

Meanwhile, put a large non-stick frying pan over a medium heat, add half the butter cubes, and heat until melted and frothy. Break the eggs gently into the pan, taking care not to burn your fingers or break the yolks. Season the whites lightly with a sprinkle of salt. Fry the eggs for 3–4 minutes until the yolks are just set, adding the remaining cubes of butter halfway.

Remove the eggs from the pan with a slotted spatula, drain, and place on the griddled side of the bottom piece of bread. Sprinkle with pepper and drizzle with ketchup. Top with the bread lid, griddled-side down, and cut in half. Eat straightaway.

KEY TO PERFECTION

When you're frying eggs, especially when there are several together in the same pan, it's tricky to get the yolks and whites cooked at the same time – the whites always set before the yolks. The trick is knowing how to speed up the cooking of the yolks.

As soon as the egg whites have set and the second lot of butter has melted, tilt the pan and spoon the hot butter over the egg yolks. Keep basting until an opaque white film sets over the yolks. This tells you that the yolks are done.

"Don't sprinkle salt on the egg yolks before or during cooking. It will make them speckly, and they won't cook evenly."

CLASSIC FRENCH OMELETTE

One of the first things you learn at catering college is how to cook an omelette, and a key question in the theory exam is: "What is the meaning of the word *baveuse*?" The answer is "cooked until moist in the centre", which is the perfect description for a perfect omelette.

SERVES 1
3 large organic eggs
50g unsalted butter, diced
Sea salt and freshly milled black pepper

Using a fork, lightly whisk the eggs in a bowl and season with salt and pepper.

Heat a 16–18cm non-stick frying pan over a medium-high heat. Add the butter and heat until foaming, then pour in the eggs. Shake the pan so the eggs run all over the bottom, then cook and stir with a spatula for 1–2 minutes so the butter gets mixed into the eggs, and the uncooked mixture runs to the sides of the pan.

When the eggs start to look softly set, season them lightly and remove the pan from the heat.

Fold two opposite edges to the centre. Lift up one of the straight edges, then roll the omelette out of the pan onto a warmed plate. Press gently into a cigar shape with a clean cloth. Sprinkle with black pepper and serve straightaway.

"If you're nervous of folding and rolling the omelette, just fold it in half to serve."

KEY TO PERFECTION

A classic French omelette should be the shape of a fat cigar, and it should ooze creaminess when you cut into it. To achieve this result, there are three key stages.

Whisk the eggs just until the yolks and whites are combined. Don't whisk too hard or you'll incorporate air, which would make the omelette tough.

Cook the eggs quickly and briefly – just until they are lightly set on the bottom but still runny on top. Don't be tempted to continue cooking or you'll lose the creamy consistency that is *baveuse*.

To get the characteristic shape of a classic French omelette, cover it with a cloth after rolling it onto the plate, then tuck the cloth in closely along the sides and press gently.

POACHED EGGS

I learnt how to poach eggs this way when I was training on the soups and eggs section at The Savoy. Every morning I'd watch the breakfast chef make them, and for every order they came out tip-top immaculate.

SERVES 2–4
4 large organic eggs
About ¹/₂tsp white wine vinegar or malt vinegar
Sea salt and freshly cracked black pepper

TO SERVE
4 muffins
Unsalted butter, for spreading

Get a bowl of water with ice cubes ready and set it aside. Fill a medium saucepan with water and bring to the boil. Meanwhile, crack one of the eggs into a small bowl or jug and add a drop of vinegar.

Whisk the boiling water to get it swirling, then slide the egg into the centre. Turn the heat down to low and poach gently for 3 minutes. Remove the egg with a slotted spoon and lower it into the ice bath.

Repeat with the remaining eggs, poaching them one at a time and scooping any scum from the surface of the water after each one. When the last egg is in the ice bath, wait for about 5 minutes for it to cool down, then lift out the eggs one at a time with the slotted spoon and . trim around the whites with scissors. Drain on a cloth. (You can leave them like this, covered with cling film, for up to 24 hours in the fridge.)

When ready to serve, bring a saucepan of water to a gentle simmer. Meanwhile, cut a thin slice off the tops of the muffins, toast on both sides, and spread with butter. Keep warm.

Gently reheat all 4 eggs together in the simmering water, allowing 2 minutes from the moment they are all in the pan. Lift them out, drain on a cloth or kitchen paper, and place on the muffins. Sprinkle with salt and pepper, and serve straightaway.

ALL IS NOT LOST
If you overcook the eggs, chop them roughly and mix with chopped mustard and cress, mayonnaise or salad cream, and seasoning. This will make a perfect sandwich filling.

KEY TO PERFECTION

Both cooking and presentation are very important with poached eggs, as all too often they can be overcooked or look messy. The method in this recipe is a clever one, and easier than you think.

Whisk the boiling water vigorously, to create a whirlpool in the centre. This will help keep the egg in shape when it first goes in.

Slip the egg into the whirlpool, then quickly lower the heat to a gentle simmer – don't let the water boil over or the egg will be spoilt.

As soon as the poached eggs are in the ice bath, they will stop cooking, and the yolks will stay runny.

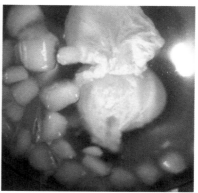

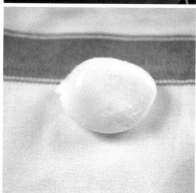

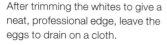

After trimming the whites to give a neat, professional edge, leave the eggs to drain on a cloth.

OMELETTE ARNOLD BENNETT

This omelette has a fascinating history. The writer Arnold Bennett had a long stay at The Savoy in 1929, doing research for his novel *The Imperial Palace*. He asked the chef for a smoked haddock and cheese omelette so often that they named the dish after him. It was an open rather than a folded omelette, and it had become such a classic at the hotel over the years that it was the first thing I put on the menu when I took over at the Savoy Grill.

SERVES 4
250g undyed smoked
haddock fillet, skinned
About 300ml full-fat milk
8 large organic eggs
50g unsalted butter, diced
40g mature Cheddar or
Gruyère cheese, grated
4tbsp double cream,
lightly whipped

FOR THE HOLLANDAISE SAUCE
250g unsalted butter, diced
100ml white wine vinegar
Juice of ¹/₂ lemon
3 large organic egg yolks
Sea salt and cracked
black pepper

First make the hollandaise sauce. Gently melt the butter in a small pan until the sediment sinks to the bottom. Pour the clear butter slowly into a jug, leaving the sediment behind, and keep warm. Put the vinegar and lemon juice in another pan with a pinch each of salt and pepper. Boil until the liquid just covers the bottom of the pan (about 3tbsp). Pass through a fine sieve into a large bowl and leave to cool.

Mix the egg yolks into the vinegar reduction and set the bowl over a pan of simmering water (a bain marie). Whisk vigorously for about 5 minutes until thick and creamy white. Remove from the heat and gradually whisk in the melted butter, leaving behind any sediment in the bottom of the jug. Set aside in a warm place.

Put the haddock in a pan with enough milk to cover. Poach gently for 5 minutes. Remove the fish with a slotted spoon and drain, then flake into large chunks, discarding any bones. Divide half of the chunks equally among four individual baking dishes. Keep warm.

Get the grill hot.

Lightly whisk 4 of the eggs with salt and pepper. Heat a large, non-stick frying pan over a low heat until hot. Add 25g of the butter and, when hot, scramble the eggs (page 146) for about 2 minutes until soft and sloppy. Divide the scrambled egg among the dishes, spooning it over the fish, then dot the remaining fish on top.

Season and lightly whisk the remaining eggs. Heat the remaining butter and scramble the eggs as before, then spoon them over the fish and smooth the top with the back of a spoon. Cover each serving with one-quarter of the grated cheese.

Fold the whipped cream into the hollandaise, dollop on top of each dish, and smooth over with the back of a spoon. Glaze the tops under the grill, and serve straightaway.

KEY TO PERFECTION

For its signature smooth texture and buttery rich flavour, this unique dish hides a secret – hollandaise sauce. There are two key stages in the making of a perfect hollandaise.

The second stage is done off the heat, with the bowl removed from the bain marie. Very slowly pour the warm (not hot) melted butter into the egg mix, whisking the whole time so the butter is smoothly incorporated without separating. When the last of the butter has gone in, you should have a thick and creamy emulsion.

For the first stage, the egg yolks and vinegar reduction must be whisked to the right consistency. To check, lift the whisk out of the mixture and move it across the surface – it should leave a ribbon trail behind it.

ALL IS NOT LOST

If the sauce curdles, drop in a few ice cubes and whisk vigorously until smooth again.

SCOTCH PANCAKES

These have always been a favourite of mine for breakfast at the weekend. I just love making them with everyone sitting round the table waiting for them to come out of the pan. They're great doused in maple syrup, but my son, Jake, and I also like them topped with thick slices of butter.

MAKES ABOUT 36
225g plain white flour
2¹/₂tsp baking powder
¹/₂tsp fine salt
¹/₂tsp ground cinnamon
60g caster sugar
4 large organic egg yolks
500ml milk
90g unsalted butter, melted and cooled
1tsp almond extract
6 large egg whites
Vegetable oil, for frying

TO SERVE
Icing sugar
Maple syrup

Sift the flour into a large bowl with the baking powder, salt, and cinnamon. Stir in the sugar, keeping back 1tbsp for later.

Whisk the egg yolks in a medium bowl until thickened, then gradually whisk in the milk, melted butter, and almond extract.

Make a well in the dry ingredients. Slowly pour in the egg yolk mixture, whisking constantly to make a smooth batter.

Put the egg whites in a clean bowl and whisk to soft peaks, adding the reserved sugar halfway through. Fold into the batter.

Set a large, non-stick frying pan over a medium heat. Splash in a little oil to cover the bottom of the pan and heat until hot. Spoon the batter into the pan to make four pancakes, each 8–10cm in diameter. Cook for 2–2¹/₂ minutes until the underside is golden brown, then turn the pancakes over and cook for 1¹/₂–2 minutes to lightly brown the other side.

Lift the pancakes out of the pan with a spatula and serve straightaway, with sugar and syrup.

Make more pancakes in the same way, cooking them four at a time and adding more oil when necessary. They are best served straight from the pan, or as soon as possible after cooking.

KEY TO PERFECTION

The secret of great Scotch pancakes is aeration – getting air into the batter at the beginning and keeping it there while the pancakes are cooking.

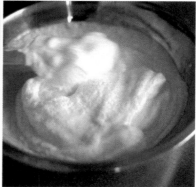

Mix a spoonful of the egg whites into the batter to loosen it slightly, then tip the rest on top of the batter and gently fold them in with a rubber spatula until evenly incorporated. Work gently and slowly to retain the air. Don't tap, whisk, or bang the bowl while you're folding or you'll knock out the air.

First, whisk the egg whites to soft, snowy peaks that are full of air. Using a balloon whisk, this should only take a minute or two – just until the peaks flop over when you stop beating.

"A bouncy, bendy balloon whisk is best for incorporating air, and it makes the job easy. Don't use a stiff, inflexible whisk or you'll have to work twice as hard."

ALL IS NOT LOST

If you leave the whisked egg whites to stand before folding them into the batter, they will split and go watery underneath. Don't worry. Throw in a small handful of sugar to stabilize the mixture, and whisk until soft peaks form again.

CRÊPES

I loved Pancake Day when I was young. It was such fun, even though Mum struggled because she didn't have the right pan. When I went to college and learnt that one of the secrets was having a good non-stick pan, I bought her one. She's never looked back.

MAKES 6
1 large organic egg
100g self-raising white flour
Pinch of fine salt
300ml full-fat milk
Vegetable oil, for frying

TO SERVE
Caster sugar
Lemon wedges

Lightly whisk the egg in a bowl, add the flour and salt, and slowly whisk in the milk. Whisk out the lumps, then strain the batter into a bowl or jug. Leave to rest for about 30 minutes in the fridge.

Put a 20cm non-stick frying pan over a medium-high heat, swirl a thin film of oil over the bottom, and heat until you can see a light haze rising.

Pour off the excess oil, then ladle in enough batter to coat the bottom of the pan in a thin layer. Put the pan back on the heat and cook the crêpe for 2–3 minutes until the underside is coloured.

Flip the crêpe over and cook the other side for 1–2 minutes, then slide the crêpe out of the pan. Serve straightaway, either rolled or folded, with sugar and lemon wedges. Continue making crêpes until all the batter is used, adding more oil when necessary.

KEY TO PERFECTION

Crêpes should be lacy thin, so you must have lump-free batter and only use a very small amount at a time. Slow but sure is the way to work.

After whisking the batter with a balloon whisk until it's as smooth as you can get it, pour it through a sieve to catch any minute lumps of flour that remain.

To cook a crêpe, tilt the pan towards you, then swish in a ladleful of batter and tilt and roll the pan from side to side. The batter should flow right to the edge. If it doesn't quite cover, fill any gaps by ladling in a little more batter.

To see if the crêpe is ready to flip over, lift up a corner and check that it is set and light golden underneath. If it is, shake the pan to release the bottom of the crêpe, and flip it over to cook the second side.

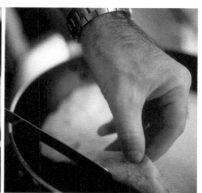

DESSERTS

VANILLA PANNACOTTA

This is one of the easiest desserts you could ever make, and virtually impossible to mess up. Here I've flavoured it with dark rum, but you could use Malibu or an orange liqueur, if that's what you've got – both of these go well with vanilla.

SERVES 4
1¹/₂ leaves gelatine
330ml double cream
50ml full-fat milk
55g caster sugar
1¹/₂ vanilla pods
¹/₂ cap dark rum

Soak the gelatine leaves in iced water for about 10 minutes until they are soft.

Meanwhile, put the cream, milk, and sugar in a heavy pan. Split the vanilla pods lengthways and scrape the seeds out into the pan, then drop in the pods. Bring to the boil, stirring occasionally. Tip in the rum and stir to mix. Take the pan off the heat.

Remove the gelatine leaves from the water and squeeze firmly. Add to the hot cream mixture, whisking until completely dissolved.

Strain the mix through a fine sieve into a jug and stand the jug in a bowl of iced water. Stir frequently until the mixture starts to thicken, then pour into four 8cm-diameter dariole moulds or ramekins. Refrigerate for 1–2 hours until set.

To serve, run the tip of a small, sharp knife around the top edge of each pannacotta to release it from the side of the mould. Dip the bottom of the mould in hot water for a few seconds, then turn the pannacotta out onto a plate.

"If you don't stir the pannacotta mix enough while it's thickening, it can set on the inside of the jug. If this happens, warm it gently by standing the jug in a pan of warm water on the stove, then cool it down again in the ice bath, stirring all the time."

KEY TO PERFECTION

Gelatine leaves give a much smoother set than gelatine powder, which can clump or be granular. They're easier to use, too.

Immerse the brittle leaves in a bowl of cold water to which you've added a few ice cubes. After about 10 minutes, the leaves will soften and become pliable.

Take the softened leaves out of the water and squeeze them tightly to get rid of as much surplus water as possible.

Drop the gelatine into the hot cream mixture while whisking constantly, or the gelatine will sink to the bottom in a clump. Keep whisking until the gelatine has completely dissolved.

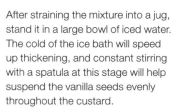

After straining the mixture into a jug, stand it in a large bowl of iced water. The cold of the ice bath will speed up thickening, and constant stirring with a spatula at this stage will help suspend the vanilla seeds evenly throughout the custard.

STRAWBERRY FOOL

When Dad brought strawberries home that were too ripe to sell to his customers (he was a fruit and potato merchant), we'd make them into purées in Mum's old mixer, then add cream or yogurt for a milk shake. This fool is almost identical, but I've added gelatine to give it a soft set.

SERVES 6
1kg soft, ripe strawberries, hulled and quartered lengthways
Juice of ½ lemon
80g caster sugar
2 leaves gelatine
250ml double cream
250g natural Greek yogurt

TO FINISH
150ml whipping cream
1tbsp sifted icing sugar

Place a large, heavy pan over a medium to high heat. When hot, put in the strawberries, lemon juice, and sugar, and cook for about 15 minutes, stirring frequently. Remove from the heat.

Soak the gelatine leaves in iced water for about 10 minutes until soft. Meanwhile, tip the contents of the pan into a blender and purée until smooth. Transfer to a large bowl.

Remove the gelatine from the water and squeeze dry, then stir into the warm purée until dissolved. Cover and refrigerate for about half an hour until chilled but not set. Lightly whip the double cream.

Stir the yogurt into the purée, then fold in the whipped cream until evenly mixed. Divide equally among six glasses. Cover and refrigerate for at least 6 hours, preferably overnight.

To finish, lightly whip the whipping cream with the icing sugar until it just holds its shape. Spoon on top of the fools. Serve straightaway or keep in the fridge for up to 2 hours before serving.

KEY TO PERFECTION

Most recipes for fruit fools have a raw purée as their base, but cooked fruit gives a smoother finish. This is simplicity itself to achieve, but often overlooked.

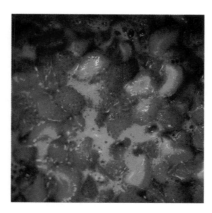

Cook the strawberries with the sugar and lemon juice until reduced down slightly, and you can see that all the pieces of fruit are very soft. Stir frequently to make sure they all cook evenly.

"Only make this fool with homegrown strawberries in season, when they're ripe and bursting with flavour. If strawberries are hard and tasteless when they're raw, they won't be any better cooked."

LEMON POSSET WITH HOT SPICED FRUITS

The idea for these spiced fruits came to me one winter when I wanted to evoke the scent and flavour of mulled wine. The extreme temperatures of hot fruits and chilled posset work really well together, and you can vary the fruit year round to suit the season.

SERVES 6
About 4 lemons
850ml double cream
250g caster sugar

FOR THE HOT SPICED FRUITS
3 stalks of rhubarb, trimmed of leaves and root ends
3 Victoria plums
A small handful of blueberries or blackcurrants (optional)
A handful each of blackberries and raspberries
50g unsalted butter, diced
150g caster sugar
2 cinnamon sticks
6 star anise
2 vanilla pods, split lengthways
3–4tbsp dark rum (optional)

Finely grate the zest from the lemons. Halve the lemons and squeeze out the juice, then strain and measure it – you need 225ml.

Mix the cream, lemon zest, and sugar in a non-stick pan. Bring to the boil, stirring occasionally until the sugar has dissolved, then simmer for 3 minutes. Take the pan off the heat and whisk in the lemon juice. Strain the mix into a jug, pressing the zest in the sieve to extract as much flavour as possible. Discard the zest.

Skim the froth off the top of the posset mix, then pour equal amounts into six whisky glasses. Leave to cool. Cover the glasses with cling film and refrigerate for at least 24 hours.

When you are ready to serve, prepare and cook the fruits. Cut the rhubarb into 1cm lozenges. Halve and stone the plums. Cut the halves lengthways down the middle and cut each quarter into four equal pieces. If using blackcurrants, top and tail them.

Heat a heavy pan over a medium heat. Add the diced butter and heat until foaming, then add the rhubarb and plums. Sauté the fruits for about 5 minutes until they start to soften, then add the blueberries or currants (if using), the sugar, cinnamon sticks, and star anise. Scrape the seeds out of the vanilla pods into the pan and drop in the pods too. Give the fruit a good stir and add the rum (if using), then cook for a further 5–8 minutes. Take the pan off the heat, remove the whole spices and vanilla pods, and fold in the blackberries and raspberries.

Serve the possets chilled, topped with the hot fruits.

KEY TO PERFECTION

The addition of a precise amount of lemon juice is crucial to the success of a posset. The acid starts off a chemical reaction in the cream, and this makes it set when it's chilled in the fridge.

An old-fashioned reamer is one of the best tools for getting the maximum juice out of a lemon. Use it over a sieve to catch all the pips and pith, then tip the strained juice into a jug and measure it accurately.

EARL GREY TEA CREAM

I got the inspiration for this dessert from tea and biscuits – I wanted to create the look and flavour of both these things together. With its subtle perfume, Earl Grey is perfect for the delicate, smooth cream, which looks exactly like a cup of tea.

SERVES 6
260ml full-fat milk
260ml double cream
7 Earl Grey teabags
80g caster sugar
95g egg yolks (from 5–6 large organic eggs)

TO SERVE
1/2 vanilla pod, cut lengthways into 6 very thin sticks
Butter Shortbread (page 202), cut into fingers

Heat the oven to 130ºC fan (150°C/gas 2).

Put the milk, cream, and teabags in a heavy pan with half of the sugar. Bring to the boil over a medium to high heat, stirring occasionally, then immediately strain through a fine sieve into a bowl, squeezing the teabags gently in the sieve.

Whisk the egg yolks in a large bowl with the remaining sugar until well combined. Pour in the tea milk and whisk well. Strain slowly through a fine sieve into another bowl, then skim to remove any foamy bubbles.

Stand six 150ml teacups or ramekins in a roasting pan. Slowly pour the tea cream into the cups (it will only fill them two-thirds full), then skim off any more bubbles. Add hot water to the roasting pan. Bake in the middle of the oven for 25–30 minutes. The tea creams are ready when their centres have a slight, but firm quiver when you shake the pan very gently. Remove the cups from the water and allow to cool.

Refrigerate the tea creams for at least 4 hours, or overnight. Serve chilled, with a vanilla stick popped into each one, and shortbread fingers.

KEY TO PERFECTION

Tea creams depend on very gentle cooking for their delicate, silky smoothness. The oven temperature is low, but you should take the added precautions of removing air bubbles from the cream mixture before cooking, and then baking in a bain marie.

Carefully skim the surface of the strained mixture using a spoon. Even one bubble can spoil the appearance of the finished cream.

Pour hot water into the roasting pan to come halfway up the sides of the cups. This bain marie will protect the tea creams from the heat of the oven, preventing them from getting too hot.

"Don't leave the teabags to stand or steep in the milk, or the tea cream will taste stewed and bitter."

CUSTARD TART

The original recipe for this tart was my nan's. She passed it on to my mum, then I made it for the Queen's 80th birthday lunch at Mansion House. I think it's as close to perfection as any custard tart can be.

CUTS INTO 6-8 SLICES
1 quantity chilled Sweet
Shortcrust Pastry (below)
2 large organic egg yolks,
lightly beaten, to glaze

FOR THE FILLING
9 large organic egg yolks
75g caster sugar
500ml whipping cream
1 whole nutmeg, for grating

Line a large roasting pan with non-stick baking parchment. Place a buttered 18 x 3.5cm pastry ring (or loose-bottomed tart tin) in the centre. Roll out the pastry and chill for half an hour, then use to line the ring, letting the surplus hang over the top. Chill for half an hour.

Heat the oven to 170°C fan (190°C/gas 5).

Bake the pastry case blind for 10 minutes until it starts to turn golden brown. Remove the paper and rice, and brush inside the pastry case with the egg yolks. Return to the oven to bake for 5 minutes. Leave to cool. Turn the oven down to 130°C fan (150°C/gas 2).

Next make the filling. Put the egg yolks and sugar in a bowl and whisk to combine. Pour in the cream and mix well, then strain the mixture through a fine sieve into a heavy pan. Warm over a low heat to blood temperature (37°C), stirring all the time. Pour into a jug.

Put the cooled pastry case, still in the ring in the parchment-lined pan, on the middle shelf of the oven. Slowly and carefully pour in the custard, filling the case as full as you can – right to the very top. Grate nutmeg liberally all over, to cover the custard completely.

Bake the tart for 45–50 minutes until the custard looks set but not firm – it should have a slight, even quiver across the top when you gently shake the roasting pan. Leave to cool to room temperature, then remove the ring. Cut into neat wedges with a sharp knife to serve.

SWEET SHORTCRUST PASTRY

230g plain white flour, sifted with
a pinch of fine salt
150g chilled unsalted butter,
diced
75g caster sugar
Finely grated zest of 1 lemon
1 medium organic egg beaten
with 1 medium organic egg yolk

In a large bowl, gently work the flour and butter together until the mix looks like breadcrumbs. Stir in the sugar and lemon zest, then add the eggs slowly to form a dough. Gently shape it into a ball and flatten slightly, then wrap tightly in cling film and refrigerate for 2 hours before using. This pastry is very fragile, and handles best when well chilled, but the end result is well worth the care and time taken.

KEY TO PERFECTION

Crisp, melt-in-the-mouth pastry is the hallmark of this traditional English tart. The trick is to get both the pastry and the pastry case right. If there are any holes or cracks, the filling will ooze out during baking and make the pastry wet.

Start making the pastry by adding the butter in small pieces to the flour and salt, picking up the butter and flour mixture and letting it roll through your fingers. Repeat, gently rubbing with your fingers, until all the butter is incorporated with the flour and the mix looks like breadcrumbs.

Mix in the sugar, lemon zest, and eggs with one hand, stroking the mixture and turning the bowl at the same time. As soon as the pastry comes together, turn it out onto a well-floured surface. Shape it gently into a ball, then pat lightly to flatten. Don't overwork it.

With a well-floured rolling pin, roll out the pastry on a well-floured surface until 3mm thick. Don't stretch the pastry while rolling, but keep turning it round and patting in the edges with floured hands until you have a disc about 8cm larger than the pastry ring. Place the disc between two sheets of floured greaseproof paper; chill for half an hour.

Roll some pastry trimmings into a ball and dust with flour, then press the ball into the bottom inside edge of the pastry case and up the side to make them smooth. If there are any cracks, press them together with your fingers. Chill again for half an hour.

Trim the edge of the disc to make it neat, then lift it on the rolling pin and drop into the ring. Ease in gently with floured hands, letting the pastry hang over the top and down the outside of the ring.

Set the shape of the pastry case by baking it blind: line it with a large sheet of greaseproof paper, fill with uncooked rice, and put it in the oven to bake for 10 minutes.

After 10 minutes, remove the paper and rice, then brush all over the inside of the pastry case with beaten egg yolk. Bake for a further 5 minutes. This will seal the pastry so the filling can't seep into it and make it soggy.

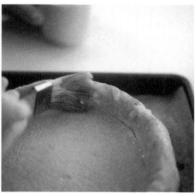

When the pastry case is cool enough to handle, it's ready to be filled. It will be crisp and golden, both inside and out.

To release the pastry from the ring before serving the tart, work around the top edge with a serrated knife using a sawing action – the excess pastry will drop away and then you can lift the ring straight up and off.

ALL IS NOT LOST

If cracks appear in the pastry case during baking blind, don't leave them or the filling will ooze out. Patch up the cracks with scraps of raw pastry and bake for an additional 5 minutes.

TREACLE TART

When my nan sent me to the cake shop to buy bread, she always told me to treat myself to a cake. I usually bought a vanilla slice or an egg custard – I was never a treacle tart fan. All that changed when I worked at The Point in the US and discovered tarts like this one. It's deep and moist, and very treacly – great with a cup of tea.

CUTS INTO 10–12 SLICES
1 quantity chilled Sweet
Shortcrust Pastry (page 172)
2 large organic egg yolks,
lightly beaten, to glaze

FOR THE FILLING
454g can golden syrup
75g finely ground almonds
115g fine fresh breadcrumbs
2 medium organic eggs, beaten
165ml double cream

Mix all the filling ingredients in a large bowl until well combined. Cover and refrigerate overnight.

Line a baking sheet with non-stick baking parchment. Put a buttered 25 x 3.5cm flan ring in the centre. Roll out the pastry on a well-floured surface to a disc about 8cm larger than the ring, then chill between two sheets of floured greaseproof paper for half an hour. Line the ring with the pastry disc (page 173), pressing it smoothly into the bottom inside edge and up the side, and letting it hang over the top and down the outside of the ring. Chill for another half an hour.

Heat the oven to 170°C fan (190°C/gas 5).

Bake the pastry case blind for 10 minutes (page 174) until it starts to turn golden brown. Remove the paper and rice, brush the inside of the pastry case with the egg yolks, and return to the oven to bake for a further 5 minutes. Leave to cool. Keep the oven on at the same temperature.

Stir the filling, then pour it into the cooled pastry case. Leave to settle for a few minutes, then place the tart in the middle of the oven and bake for 10 minutes.

Turn the oven down to 150°C fan (170°C/gas 3) and bake for a further 35 minutes until the filling is a deep caramel brown, and firm when gently touched in the middle.

Leave the tart to settle for 10–15 minutes, then saw off the overhanging pastry using a serrated knife. Carefully lift off the flan ring. Serve the tart warm or cold.

"If you haven't got a 25cm flan ring, you can use a loose-bottomed tart tin instead."

KEY TO PERFECTION

The filling must be made the day before baking to allow time for the breadcrumbs to absorb the golden syrup and swell, and the pastry case must be partially baked before the filling goes in. These are the secrets of a deep-filled and moist treacle tart with crisp, sweet pastry.

When you stir the filling ingredients together at the start, the mixture will be thin and runny.

After chilling in the fridge overnight, stir the filling again. It will be very thick.

Pour the thickened filling into the partially baked pastry case, then place in the oven to bake until richly coloured.

DEEP-DISH APPLE PIE

I always make apple pie this way, with two different types of apples. I use tart cooking apples that break down to make a firm compote base, and sweet eating apples that retain their shape so the slices sit pretty on top. With its crisp, buttery pastry, it's sheer perfection.

CUTS INTO 8–10 SLICES
1 quantity chilled Sweet Shortcrust Pastry (page 172)
100g caster sugar mixed with 20g ground cinnamon
1 large organic egg white, lightly beaten

FOR THE FILLING
6 large Bramley apples (about 1.5kg total weight)
30g unsalted butter, diced
2–3 cinnamon sticks, broken into large pieces
150g caster sugar
5 medium Braeburn or Pink Lady apples

Peel, quarter, and core the Bramley apples, then chop into small pieces. Warm a large, heavy pan over a medium heat. Add the butter and wait until it starts to foam, then add the cinnamon sticks and sauté for 2–3 minutes to get the spicy aroma going. Add the apple pieces and the sugar, and cook uncovered for about 20 minutes until fairly dry, stirring occasionally. Tip the apple compote out of the pan and spread over a large platter or tray. Leave until cold.

Meanwhile, roll out two-thirds of the pastry on a well-floured surface to 5mm thick. Use to line a loose-bottomed 20 x 5cm cake tin or springform tin, patching any cracks and letting the pastry hang over the top. Set the tin on a baking tray. Roll out the remaining pastry to make a lid 3mm thick and place between two sheets of floured greaseproof paper. Refrigerate the pastry case and lid for 1 hour.

Spread the cold compote in the chilled pastry case, discarding the cinnamon. Peel the Braeburn apples, halve them lengthways, and cut out the cores. Slice the apples 3mm thick. Arrange the apple slices overlapping on top of the compote, spiralling them in from the edge and doming them in the centre. Sprinkle them with some of the cinnamon sugar as you are layering them up.

Brush the edge of the pastry case with egg white. Place the chilled pastry lid carefully on top and press to seal the edges together. Trim and fork around the edge, and cut two or three slits in the centre of the lid. Refrigerate for 1 hour.

Heat the oven to 180°C fan (200°C/gas 6).

Brush the pie lid with egg white and sprinkle with some of the remaining cinnamon sugar, then bake on the tray for 55–60 minutes, covering the top with foil if it becomes too brown. Leave the pie to rest for about half an hour before removing it from the tin. Sprinkle with more cinnamon sugar before serving.

KEY TO PERFECTION

The Bramley apple compote needs to be quite dry. If it is wet,
it will seep into the pastry base and make the pie soggy.

Start cooking the Bramley apple
pieces over a medium heat with the
butter, cinnamon, and sugar – they
will soon break down to a pulp.

Just before the end of the cooking
time, increase the heat to high and
stir vigorously – this will drive off the
moisture and help the compote
become thick and dry.

*"To turn this pie into a tart, make
the pastry case slightly thicker and
leave the lid off. The tart will cook
in about two-thirds of the time."*

NEW YORK CHEESECAKE

This is the real thing – baked, rich, and creamy – just what you'd expect if you went to New York. It's perfect plain, but to cut through the richness I sometimes serve it with an American-style blueberry compote, to which I add a little lemon juice to sharpen the taste.

CUTS INTO 8–10 SLICES
60g unsalted butter, melted and cooled
135g plain digestive biscuits, crushed into crumbs
500g full-fat soft cheese, at room temperature
200g caster sugar
5tbsp double cream
30g cornflour
4 large organic eggs, beaten

Heat the oven to 100ºC fan (120°C/gas ¼). Put a loose-bottomed 20 x 5cm cake tin or springform tin on a baking tray.

Mix the melted butter through the crushed biscuits. Press over the bottom of the tin to make a smooth, even layer that goes tight into the edge.

Put the soft cheese in a bowl and mix in the sugar, cream, and cornflour using a rubber spatula. Pour in the eggs and beat together until really smooth.

Pour the mix over the biscuit base. Shake the tin to level the filling and smooth the top.

Bake the cheesecake on the middle shelf of the oven for 1½ hours until just set but still with a little wobble in the centre. Allow to cool to room temperature before removing the side from the tin.

KEY TO PERFECTION

Baked cheesecakes are richer and more satisfying than cheesecakes set with gelatine, which tend to be light and fluffy. To get the dreamy, creamy texture that makes a baked cheesecake so special, you need to pay attention to detail before baking.

The cheese filling must be well mixed so there are no lumps. It will then pour evenly over the biscuit base, which must be flat.

Once the filling is level in the tin, smooth over the top with your fingertip to remove any air bubbles. This will prevent uneven rising, so the top of the cheesecake will bake perfectly flat.

"Always use a full-fat cheese for this classic American cheesecake – low-fat cheese won't give the right creamy texture – and don't refrigerate the cheesecake or it will go rock solid."

CREAMY RICE PUDDING

I don't like the sort of rice pudding that's cooked in the oven and has a thick skin on top, but I have to confess that I do like creamed rice pudding from a tin. This is my extra-rich, homemade version – it's definitely not the kind you had at school.

SERVES 4
90g short-grain pudding rice
250ml full-fat milk
250ml double cream
1 vanilla pod, split lengthways, and seeds scraped out and reserved
5 medium organic egg yolks
90g caster sugar
Jam, to serve

Rinse and drain the rice, then tip into a heavy pan. Pour in the milk and cream and drop in the vanilla pod (not the seeds). Bring to the boil over a medium heat, stirring occasionally. Turn the heat down to low and simmer gently, stirring from time to time, for about 20 minutes until the rice is soft but still with a slight bite.

Put the egg yolks in a bowl with the sugar and vanilla seeds, and whisk to combine.

Take the pan of rice from the heat and remove the vanilla pod. Mix about one-third of the rice with the egg yolks, then stir this mix into the rest of the rice in the pan. Continue cooking over a low heat for a few more minutes, stirring constantly, until the pudding is thick enough to coat the back of the spoon.

Pour the pudding into bowls and blob a spoonful of jam in the centre of each. If you like, give the rice a baked look by flashing a blowtorch briefly over the top. Serve hot.

"This rice pudding is so rich and creamy that it's just as good cold as hot. For a change from jam, try serving it with warmed, sliced apricots or peaches topped with a sprinkling of cinnamon and toasted flaked almonds."

KEY TO PERFECTION

Egg yolks make this rice pudding wonderfully thick, rich, and creamy, but you must prevent them from overheating or they might curdle.

Don't add the egg yolk mixture to the hot rice all in one go. Instead, take the pan off the heat and make a *liaison* by slowly whisking one-third of the hot rice into the egg yolk mixture a spoonful at a time. This is called "letting down", and it helps prevent the yolks from curdling.

With the pan back on the heat, stir the egg yolk *liaison* into the rice pudding in the pan. Use a wooden spatula and stir continuously to stop the pudding sticking to the bottom. Stirring also keeps the mixture on the move, which helps prevent the liquid from overheating and curdling.

When you can draw a finger smoothly through the pudding coating the back of the spatula, you know the egg yolks have done their job.

ALL IS NOT LOST

If you've let the pudding get too hot and you can see it starting to separate, whip the pan off the heat and quickly beat in a splash of cold cream. This will cool the pudding down and stop it curdling.

TREACLE SPONGE

Dad used to bulk-buy treacle sponge in tins. It would sit in the pantry for ages until he forced us to eat it because it was getting close to its "best before" date. It was far too sweet and stodgy for me – this sponge pudding is lighter, and very moist.

SERVES 4–6

200g golden syrup, plus extra warmed syrup to serve
Finely grated zest of 2 small oranges
Juice of 1 small orange (about 50ml)
175g softened unsalted butter, plus extra for the bowl
175g light soft brown sugar
3 large organic eggs, beaten
1tsp black treacle
175g self-raising white flour, sifted

Brush a 1-litre pudding bowl with butter. Mix the golden syrup with the orange zest and juice, and pour into the bottom of the bowl.

Beat the butter and sugar together until light and fluffy, using an electric mixer or a wooden spoon. Slowly add the eggs, beating well. Add the treacle, then fold in the flour until evenly mixed.

Spoon the batter into the bowl and smooth the top. Don't worry when the syrup oozes up the side – this will make the pudding moist. Cover tightly and steam in a covered pan half filled with boiling water for 2 hours, checking the water level regularly to prevent boiling dry.

Uncover the pudding and turn it out onto a plate. Pour warmed golden syrup over the top and serve straightaway.

KEY TO PERFECTION

It's essential to cover the bowl properly before steaming, both to allow room for the pudding to rise, and to prevent water and steam from getting into the mixture and making it unpleasantly soggy.

Make a greaseproof paper cartouche (page 88) that is 5cm larger than the top of the bowl. Lay the cartouche over the top of the bowl and fold a deep pleat in the centre.

Fold the cartouche down over the edge of the bowl and tie it securely under the rim with string.

Lay a large sheet of foil over the cartouche, then crumple and fold it under the rim to seal.

CRUMBLE AND CUSTARD

I'm often asked how to make a nice deep crumble without it getting soggy from the fruit underneath. The answer is simple – cook the fruit and crumble separately. In fact, I like the crumble part so much that I often give the fruit a miss altogether, as I've done here.

SERVES 6
165g unsalted butter,
slightly softened
165g demerara sugar
270g plain white flour, sifted
100–150g hazelnuts, toasted
and chopped

FOR THE CUSTARD
6 large organic egg yolks
60g caster sugar
2tsp custard powder
250ml full-fat milk
250ml double cream
1 vanilla pod

Heat the oven to 180°C fan (200°C/gas 6).

First make the crumble. Rub the butter, sugar, and flour together in a bowl with your fingertips until the mix looks like coarse breadcrumbs. Stir in the hazelnuts. Press the mixture evenly over a large baking tray (about 33 x 23cm), then bake for 30–35 minutes until crisp and golden.

Meanwhile, make the custard. Whisk the egg yolks, sugar, and custard powder in a large bowl, then set aside. Pour the milk and cream into a heavy pan. Split the vanilla pod in half lengthways, scrape the seeds into the pan, and drop in the pod too. Bring to the boil.

Slowly whisk the hot milk and cream into the custard powder mixture, then pour back into the pan and bring to the boil, stirring with a spatula. Cook over a low to medium heat for about 5 minutes until thickened, stirring constantly with the spatula and scraping it round the bottom and edge of the pan.

Break the crumble into rough pieces and divide among six bowls. Strain the hot custard into a jug. Pour over the crumble and serve.

KEY TO PERFECTION

Using custard powder stabilizes the egg yolks so the custard can be heated to boiling without curdling. This makes a soothing, steaming hot custard with no floury taste.

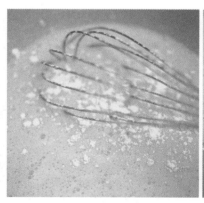

Whisk the egg yolks and sugar together first, then sprinkle the custard powder over the top. If the powder goes in too soon, it will be difficult to get rid of any lumps.

Continue whisking vigorously until smooth. If not used straightaway, whisk the mixture again before adding the hot milk and cream.

CHOCOLATE FONDANTS

My first experience of eating this wickedly rich dessert was when Jean-Georges Vongerichten opened Vong in London. Sadly, the restaurant is long gone, but the memory of their chocolate fondants is still incredibly vivid.

SERVES 6
2 medium organic eggs,
at room temperature
2 medium organic egg yolks,
at room temperature
120g caster sugar
90g good-quality dark
chocolate (at least 70%
cocoa solids), finely chopped
90g softened unsalted butter
45g plain white flour, sifted

Butter the inside of six metal rings that are 5cm in diameter and 4–5cm tall. Line each ring with non-stick baking parchment to come just above the top. Stand them on a parchment-lined baking sheet.

Whisk the whole eggs in a bowl, add the egg yolks and sugar, and whisk again until evenly combined.

Melt the chocolate and butter very gently in a bowl set over a pan of hot water (a bain marie). Remove the bowl from the pan and stir the chocolate gently. Cool for a minute or two, then whisk the chocolate into the egg mixture. Add the flour and whisk well to ensure there are no lumps. Chill for 30 minutes.

Spoon the mixture into the parchment-lined rings, filling them about two-thirds full. Refrigerate for 3–4 hours until set.

Heat the oven to 180°C fan (200°C/gas 6).

Bake the fondants in the middle of the oven for 10 minutes. Remove from the oven and allow to rest for 2 minutes, then very carefully lift the metal rings up and off, and gently peel off the parchment. With a spatula, transfer the fondants to small plates, taking care not to puncture them as they are soft. Serve straightaway.

"If you haven't got small metal rings, you can make and serve these fondants in 150ml ramekins."

KEY TO PERFECTION

For fondants to have their signature gooey centres, you must handle the chocolate with gentle care. If it becomes too hot during melting, or if water gets into it, the chocolate can become grainy or "seize" into a hard lump.

Both the egg mixture and the melted chocolate must be at the same temperature when they are whisked together. If the eggs are cold, or taken straight from the fridge, they will make the chocolate "split" and look grainy.

Melt the chocolate and butter in a bain marie. Make sure the heat under the pan is low, and that the base of the bowl is not touching the water. A bowl with a lip that fits snugly over the pan is best, to prevent moisture from seeping up the sides into the chocolate.

ALL IS NOT LOST

If the chocolate sets in a hard ball or becomes grainy, you can't use it for the fondants, but you can easily turn it into truffles. Stir in 100ml double cream, then pour into a deep tray and chill until set. Roll into balls, or scoop with a melon baller dipped in hot water, and roll in cocoa powder. Chill until firm, then roll in more cocoa powder.

MINI MERINGUES

Darren, my old head chef at Pétrus, made these at the drop of a hat one New Year's Eve, when something went wrong in the pâtisserie department. Quick and simple, they can be served as a dessert or petit four, and they're great for parties.

MAKES ABOUT 25
A wedge of lemon
100g egg whites (from
about 3 large organic eggs)
200g caster sugar

FOR THE FILLING
200g good-quality dark
chocolate (at least 70%
cocoa solids), finely chopped
200ml double cream
20g icing sugar, sifted

Heat the oven to 100°C fan (120°C/gas ¼). Line two large baking sheets (each about 40 x 30cm) with non-stick baking parchment.

Rub a lemon wedge over the inside of your electric mixer bowl. Put the egg whites in the bowl and whisk to soft peaks on low to medium speed. Increase the speed to high and continue whisking, adding the sugar gradually until the meringue is stiff.

Pipe twenty-five 5cm rosettes of meringue on each parchment-lined baking sheet, using a piping bag fitted with a large star nozzle. Bake for 1 hour until firm and crisp, swapping the baking sheets over halfway through baking. Lift the meringues, still on their parchment sheets, off the baking sheets and leave to cool. Line the baking sheets with clean parchment.

Meanwhile, make the filling. Melt the chocolate in a bain marie (pages 190–191), then remove from the heat. Dip the flat base of each meringue in the chocolate, then place them chocolate-side down on the clean parchment. Leave to set in the fridge.

Whip the cream with the icing sugar until firm. Use to sandwich the meringues together in pairs, chocolate sides into the centre. Serve straightaway or keep in the fridge for up to 2 hours.

"If you can spare the time, let the meringues dry out for about 4 hours after baking and before filling. This will crisp them up."

KEY TO PERFECTION

For meringues to be light and crisp, and not at all grainy, the egg whites should be whisked in two stages, and the caster sugar should be added little by little to make sure that plenty of air is beaten in.

Before starting to whisk, wipe round the inside of the bowl with the cut side of a lemon wedge. This will ensure that the bowl is clean and free of grease – essential for the egg whites to stiffen when whisked.

Whisk the egg whites on their own to the soft peak stage. They should be floppy, and still quite wet.

Add the sugar to the partially whisked egg whites a heaped large spoonful at a time, whisking for a minute after each addition. When all of the sugar has been added, the meringue should be glossy and stand in stiff peaks when the whisk is lifted out.

ALL IS NOT LOST

If you break the meringues when you lift them off the tray, or if you have any left over, you can make them into Eton Mess. Crumble them roughly into a bowl, then fold in whipped cream and crushed strawberries (the amounts of these are up to you). Serve within 1–2 hours, otherwise the meringues will lose their crispness.

"I've got a range cooker so I can fit all the meringues on one very wide oven tray. This saves having to swap over baking sheets halfway."

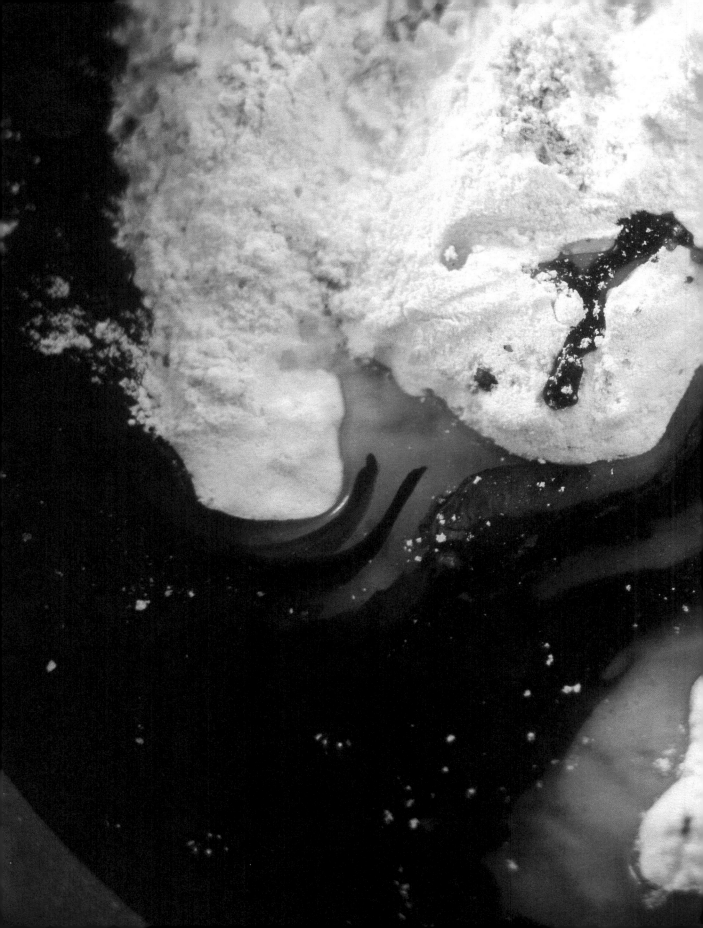

BAKING

BANANA BREAD

My wife often makes this for our boys, as it's incredibly quick and simple to do, and they're just mad about bananas. Like me, they'd eat bananas and custard every day of the week if they could, which is why we've always got bananas in the fruit bowl.

CUTS INTO 10–12 SLICES
2 large organic eggs
1tsp vanilla extract
1tsp almond extract
300g strong white bread flour
1tsp baking powder
¼tsp fine salt
115g softened unsalted butter,
plus extra for the tin
100g caster sugar
4 overripe bananas
(about 550g total weight),
peeled and mashed
75g walnuts, chopped

Heat the oven to 180°C fan (200°C/gas 6). Brush a 1kg loaf tin with butter and line the bottom with non-stick baking parchment.

Beat the eggs in a jug with the vanilla and almond extracts. Sift the flour into a bowl with the baking powder and salt.

Cream the butter and sugar together until light and fluffy, using the paddle attachment of an electric mixer on high speed. With the machine at low speed, slowly pour in the eggs, beating until they are completely incorporated (don't worry if the mix looks split at this point – it will come together later). Turn the machine off.

Mix in the mashed bananas, then fold in the sifted dry ingredients and the walnuts one-third at a time, just until the ingredients come together. Pour into the loaf tin and place on a baking sheet. Bake in the middle of the oven for 55 minutes until firm to the touch but still a little moist in the centre.

Cool in the tin for about 15 minutes, then turn out onto a wire rack and peel off the parchment. Leave until cold before slicing.

"If you've got black or spotty, overripe bananas and no time to make this bread, put the bananas in the freezer. They will keep for months, and you can also use them to make great smoothies."

KEY TO PERFECTION

Overripe bananas with black, spotted skins are essential for this bread to taste good and have a moist texture. Don't try to make it with underripe or yellow bananas because they won't mash, mix, or bake well, and be careful not to overcook the bread or you will make it dry.

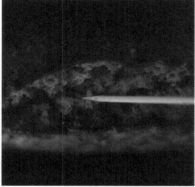

To test if the bread is done, insert a skewer in the centre. With most cake mixtures the skewer should come out clean, but a perfectly cooked banana bread will have some moist mixture clinging to it.

Mash the bananas with a fork until they're a loose, creamy consistency that will blend well with the other ingredients. This will be an easy job if the bananas are overripe because they'll offer no resistance. From 550g bananas in their skins, you'll get about 400g mashed flesh.

IRISH SODA BREAD

Richard Corrigan makes the best soda bread in London at his restaurant Bentley's in Piccadilly, so I asked him for the recipe. This is my version, and it's great served in thick chunks with plenty of unsalted butter.

MAKES 2 LOAVES
100g plain wholemeal flour, plus extra for dusting
100g self-raising white flour
1tbsp bicarbonate of soda
50g large oat flakes
25g wheat germ
25g wheat bran
1¼tsp fine salt
5tbsp clear honey
1½tbsp black treacle
225ml buttermilk

Heat the oven to 160°C fan (180°C/gas 4). Line a baking sheet with non-stick baking parchment and dust with flour.

Mix all the dry ingredients together in a large bowl. Add the honey, treacle, and buttermilk, and mix together with your hands until you have a soft dough.

Turn the dough out onto a floured surface and divide in half with floured hands. Shape each half into a ball. Place on the baking sheet and flatten slightly.

Bake in the middle of the oven for 30 minutes until the breads sound hollow when they are tapped on the base. Cool on a wire rack.

KEY TO PERFECTION

Breads made with yeast must be kneaded well to develop the gluten in the flour or they won't rise. Soda bread has no yeast, so it requires hardly any work. In fact, you should handle the dough as little as possible – and the faster you mix the better.

When there are raising agents like bicarbonate of soda and self-raising flour in a dough, they are activated as soon as liquid is added. Work fast, mixing the ingredients lightly and quickly with your hands.

As soon as the dough starts to come together as a rough mass, stop mixing and tip it out of the bowl. Never overmix this type of dough or the raising agents will get tired and won't work.

Shape the dough roughly – there's no need for a tin – and get it into the oven straightaway. That's the beauty of soda bread – you don't have to wait for it to rise before baking.

BUTTER SHORTBREAD

This recipe was given to me by my wife's mum, Doreen. She cuts the shortbread into chunky pieces as I've done here, but in the restaurant I make slim, dainty shortbread fingers – you can see them with the Earl Grey Tea Cream on page 171.

MAKES ABOUT 20 PIECES
200g plain white flour
Pinch of fine salt
40g ground rice
75g caster sugar,
plus extra for dusting
175g unsalted butter, from
a chilled 250g block

Sift the flour and salt into a bowl and stir in the ground rice and sugar. Grate in the butter, then work it quickly into the flour until the mixture resembles fine breadcrumbs.

Press the mix into a 20cm square baking tin and level the top. Chill in the fridge for about an hour.

Heat the oven to 140°C fan (160°C/gas 3).

Bake the shortbread for 40 minutes until light golden. Remove from the oven and prick all over with a fork, then mark into 20 pieces, cutting right through to the bottom of the tin. Dust liberally with caster sugar, then leave to cool before removing from the tin.

KEY TO PERFECTION

For buttery, melt-in-the-mouth shortbread, you need to work lightly and quickly. The less you handle the ingredients during mixing the better.

Put the bowl of dry ingredients on the scales, return the dial to zero, and grate in 175g butter from the chilled 250g block. By grating the butter, you hardly have to touch it.

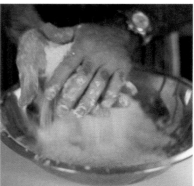

Mix the butter into the flour by rolling the two together lightly between the palms of your hands. As the butter is grated into tiny pieces, the work's virtually done for you.

CHOCOLATE CAKE

To my mind this is the best chocolate cake ever, and it's a real family recipe. It was handed down to my wife's mum, Doreen, by her mother, Elsie, and now Doreen has passed it on to us. To keep the tradition going, we use their buttercream filling and icing too, and always top the cake with flaked almonds.

CUTS INTO 8–10 SLICES
225g self-raising white flour
25g cocoa powder
Pinch of fine salt
250g softened unsalted butter, plus extra for the tins
250g caster sugar
4 large organic eggs, beaten

TO FINISH
200g icing sugar
4tbsp cocoa powder
100g softened unsalted butter
A little milk (about 1tbsp)
A handful of flaked almonds

Heat the oven to 170ºC fan (190°C/gas 5). Brush two 20 x 3.5cm round cake tins with softened butter and line the bottom and sides with non-stick baking parchment. Sift the flour, cocoa powder, and salt into a bowl. Set aside.

Cream the butter with the sugar until light and fluffy, using the paddle attachment of an electric mixer on high speed. Turn the speed down to low, then add the eggs a little at a time. Turn the machine off. Using a rubber spatula or a large metal spoon, fold in the flour and cocoa mixture one-third at a time until evenly incorporated.

Divide the mixture equally between the tins and smooth the tops. Place in the centre of the oven (preferably on the same shelf) and bake for 25 minutes. The cakes are done when a skewer inserted in the centre comes out clean. Leave to cool in the tins for 10 minutes, remove, and cool on a wire rack before peeling off the parchment.

To finish the cake, sift the icing sugar and 2tbsp of the cocoa powder into a bowl and beat in the butter to make a smooth and fluffy buttercream icing. Sandwich the cakes together with two-thirds of the icing. Sift the remaining cocoa powder into the rest of the icing and soften with a little milk to make a spreading consistency. Spread on top of the cake, then sprinkle the almonds around the edge.

KEY TO PERFECTION

This dreamy chocolate cake is made by the creaming method. There are two important stages for success – the first one puts air into the mixture and the second keeps it there.

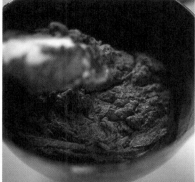

Fold the flour and cocoa into the creamed mixture using a figure of eight motion. Folding is a technique that helps keep air in the mixture so the cakes will rise during baking and be light to eat. If you beat or stir, you'll knock out the air, the cakes won't rise well, and they'll be heavy.

Cream the butter and sugar together at high speed until pale in colour and fluffy in texture. This will take about 10 minutes, and the mixture should look white, almost like whipped cream. For the cake to rise and have a light, airy texture, correct creaming is essential.

ALL IS NOT LOST

If the mix starts to look curdled when you're adding the eggs, beat in a couple of spoonfuls of the flour and cocoa. This will halt the curdling immediately, then you can carry on adding the rest of the eggs.

PINEAPPLE UPSIDE-DOWN CAKE

This was the very first thing I made in home economics lessons at school, and I remember taking it home on my bike in a biscuit tin. Later, when I was at college, my pastry lecturer, Anne Cousins, said I had a natural ability for baking, and for a while I did toy with the idea of taking it up professionally. But I've no regrets – the heat of the kitchen's the place for me.

CUTS INTO 8 SQUARES
300g self-raising white flour
Pinch of fine salt
About 3–4tbsp warmed golden syrup, plus extra for brushing
8 rings of canned pineapple (from a 425g can in syrup or natural juice), drained
11 glacé cherries
300g softened unsalted butter, plus extra for the tin
300g caster sugar
5 large organic eggs, lightly beaten

Heat the oven to 170°C fan (190°C/gas 5). Sift the flour and salt into a bowl and set aside.

Butter a 30 x 19 x 3.5cm baking tin. Line the bottom of the tin with non-stick baking parchment and brush with butter. Pour in the warm golden syrup straight from the can. With the back of the spoon, spread the syrup evenly over the parchment. Arrange the pineapple rings on the syrup in two rows of four, then place glacé cherries in the centre of the rings and in between.

Cream the butter and sugar together until light and fluffy, using the paddle attachment of an electric mixer on high speed. With the machine on low speed, slowly mix in the eggs. Turn the machine off. Using a rubber spatula or large metal spoon, fold the flour into the creamed mixture one-third at a time until completely incorporated.

Slowly pour the cake mixture over the fruit in the tin, then spread the mix smooth so that it covers the fruit completely. Bake in the middle of the oven for 45 minutes until a skewer inserted in the centre of the cake comes out clean. Leave the cake to rest in the tin on a wire rack for 5 minutes.

Run a sharp knife around the top edges of the cake to release it from the tin. Place a sheet of greaseproof paper over a wire rack, then turn the cake out onto the paper. Carefully peel away the parchment lining, taking care not to tug it and dislodge the fruit.

Brush enough warmed golden syrup over the cake to cover it liberally, then leave for a couple of minutes to let the syrup soak in. Serve the cake warm for dessert with custard or cream, or cold as a cut-and-come-again cake (it keeps well for up to a week in an airtight container).

KEY TO PERFECTION

To look its best, this cake needs attention to detail when preparing the tin and arranging the fruit in the bottom.
If you take time at this stage, your efforts will be rewarded when you turn the cake out and get a perfect-looking result.

Taking care not to dislodge the pattern, pour and spoon the cake mixture slowly in a line down each row of fruit. When all the fruit is covered, smooth over the top of the cake mixture lightly with the back of the spoon.

Pour warm, runny syrup over the softened butter on the paper, then spread it out to a thick, even layer with the back of a spoon. This will hold the fruit in place and help make the sponge nice and moist.

ENJOY COOKING

"Last but not least, relax and be confident. The food will taste better for it."

SULTANA SCONES

Before I married Jane we used to go to her house when we were courting, and her mum, Doreen, always had home-baked pastries and cakes on offer. In the evening she'd come in from the kitchen with freshly baked scones. It was a sure way to win a young man over.

MAKES ABOUT 12
450g self-raising white flour
¹/₂tsp baking powder
Pinch of fine salt
100g cold unsalted butter, diced
225ml full-fat milk
1 large organic egg, beaten
75g caster sugar
75g sultanas

Heat the oven to 200°C fan (220°C/gas 7). Line a baking tray with non-stick baking parchment.

Sift the flour, baking powder, and salt into a bowl. Rub in the butter until the mixture resembles breadcrumbs, loosely gathering the mixture together in your hands without squeezing or pressing. Stir in the sugar and sultanas.

Mix the milk and egg together, then slowly pour two-thirds into the flour, stirring constantly with a table knife until the dough comes together. It should be quite firm, but moist, so add a little more of the milk and egg if it appears too dry.

Turn the dough onto a lightly floured surface and knead briefly for only a minute or two – just long enough to be able to shape it into a rough, loose ball. Now roll it out until it's about 2cm thick. Cut out about 12 scones using a 6.5cm pastry cutter, dipping it in flour before each cut.

Place the scones on the baking tray and brush the tops lightly with the remaining egg and milk mixture. Bake in the middle of the oven for 10–15 minutes until risen and light golden brown. Serve as soon as possible, preferably while still warm.

"When Doreen comes to stay, she always makes these scones with the boys. They're such fun for children to make, and they turn out good to eat too."

KEY TO PERFECTION

Scones are very easy to make, but they need a light touch or they'll be chewy and stodgy, so work quickly and don't overhandle the dough.

Roll out the dough to 2cm thickness on a lightly floured surface. You can re-roll the trimmings and cut out more scones, but don't roll the dough any thinner or you'll have biscuits rather than scones.

FLAPJACKS

Mum used to make really thick, soft flapjacks. I liked them a lot when I was little, but now I prefer flapjacks thinner and crunchier, so I've perfected my own recipe. It's quite different from Mum's.

MAKES ABOUT 16
400g rolled oats
50g raisins, chopped
Pinch of fine salt
150g unsalted butter, plus softened butter for the tin
5tbsp soft brown sugar
4tbsp golden syrup, plus a few extra spoonfuls warmed syrup, for drizzling

Heat the oven to 150°C fan (170°C/gas 3). Brush a shallow 33 x 23cm baking tin with softened butter and line with non-stick baking parchment.

Mix the oats, raisins, and salt in a large bowl and make a well in the centre. In a heavy pan, gently melt the butter with the sugar and syrup. Pour into the well, then gradually bring the oats into the centre until everything is evenly combined.

Press the mixture into the baking tin, making sure it goes right into the corners. Bake in the middle of the oven for 25 minutes. Remove from the oven and drizzle with syrup, then return to the oven to bake for a further 10 minutes.

Cut the flapjacks into squares while hot. Leave to cool in the tin, then remove and store in an airtight container.

KEY TO PERFECTION

To make crunchy flapjacks, you need surprisingly few ingredients. The secret lies in the way they are mixed and baked.

Use your hands to quickly combine the dry ingredients with the melted butter, syrup, and sugar. The mixture should be sticky, and come together easily when squeezed.

Towards the end of baking, drizzle warmed golden syrup over the flapjack mixture, then brush it in. This is how to make the inside gooey and the top sweet and crisp.

PETIT-BROWNIES

I like my brownies to be pure gooey chocolate, with just a hint of crispness to bite through on the top. At Pétrus we serve brownies in tiny squares as petits fours, but you can cut them larger to serve as a dessert with ice cream.

MAKES ABOUT 30
300g icing sugar, plus extra for dusting
180g plain white flour
40g cocoa powder
300g good-quality dark chocolate (at least 70% cocoa solids), chopped
180g unsalted butter, diced, plus extra softened butter for the tin
4tbsp golden syrup
4 large organic eggs, beaten
2tsp vanilla extract

Heat the oven to 180ºC fan (200°C/gas 6). Brush a 30 x 20 x 3.5cm baking tin with softened butter and line the bottom and sides with non-stick baking parchment.

Sift the icing sugar, flour, and cocoa powder into a large bowl. Set aside.

Melt the chocolate in a bain marie (pages 190–191). Remove the bowl from the pan, add the butter and golden syrup, and stir until they are melted and evenly incorporated with the chocolate. Leave to cool to room temperature.

Beat the eggs and vanilla extract into the chocolate mixture, then add to the dry ingredients and beat again until smooth. Pour into the baking tin and smooth the top. Bake in the middle of the oven for 20 minutes until the top is slightly cracked and the centre feels soft and still a little moist. Leave to cool in the tin.

Turn the cake out and remove the parchment. Trim the edges to make them straight, then cut into squares. Sift icing sugar over the brownies before serving.

KEY TO PERFECTION

The secret of perfectly formed, moist brownies is in the presentation and timing. For brownies to look as good as they taste, you must pay attention to detail before baking, and take the brownies out of the oven as soon as they're done.

Undercooking is the key. To check if the brownies are done, insert the tip of a sharp knife in the centre. The knife should come out with some moist mixture clinging to it. Don't be tempted to put the brownies back in the oven.

Lay a sheet of cling film over the uncooked mixture and smooth the film out with your fingertips so there are no wrinkles or creases. Press it gently into the corners and along the sides, then carefully peel it off. The surface of the brownie mixture will be perfectly flat.

CHOCOLATE CHIP COOKIES

We keep these in a biscuit tin in the fridge at home – I love cold chocolate. When I come home from work late, it's hard not to go to the fridge and take out a cookie or two. I find them irresistible.

MAKES ABOUT 20
180g strong white bread flour
¹/₂tsp baking powder
Pinch of fine salt
115g softened unsalted butter
75g caster sugar
75g soft brown sugar
1 medium organic egg, beaten
¹/₂tsp vanilla extract
170g good-quality dark chocolate chips (at least 70% cocoa solids), or chopped dark chocolate

Sift the flour into a bowl with the baking powder and salt.

Cream the butter and both sugars together until light and fluffy, using the paddle attachment of an electric mixer on high speed. Turn the speed down to low and slowly mix in the egg. Tip in the vanilla extract. Turn the machine off. Using a rubber spatula, fold in the flour in two batches until evenly incorporated.

Fold the chocolate chips into the dough. Form into a log (about 25 x 5cm) on a lightly floured surface and wrap in cling film. Refrigerate for at least 2 hours until firm.

Heat the oven to 170ºC fan (190°C/gas 5). Line two baking trays with non-stick baking parchment.

Cut the chilled dough into about 20 slices and place them slightly apart on the baking trays. Bake for 12–15 minutes until golden brown. Cool the cookies on the trays, then keep in an airtight tin.

"The cookie dough can be stored in the fridge for up to a week, so you can slice off and bake as many cookies as you like, when you like."

KEY TO PERFECTION

The dough must be well chilled or the biscuits will spread out of shape during baking. Chilling also keeps the chocolate chips firm, so they remain chunky.

After shaping, wrap the log of dough tightly in a double layer of cling film, then refrigerate to firm it up.

When you're ready to bake, slice off as many cookies as you want – the chilled dough will cut cleanly and neatly into discs.

Space the cookies apart on the parchment-lined trays so the heat can circulate freely around them. This will also ensure that they won't spread into each other.

BLUEBERRY MUFFINS

The muffins you see in the shops look the way they do because the moulds are overfilled with mixture. I don't think it's necessary to make them so huge. Why would you want to eat all that much for breakfast anyway? Mine are the real thing – small and perfectly formed.

MAKES 18
435g plain white flour
2tsp baking powder
1tsp fine salt
³/₄tsp ground cinnamon
180g caster sugar
80g unsalted butter
230ml full-fat milk
3 medium organic eggs
100g blueberries

Heat the oven to 180°C fan (200°C/gas 6). Using paper cases, line 18 cups in two or three standard-size muffin tins.

Sift the flour into a large bowl with the baking powder, salt, and cinnamon. Stir in the sugar. Mix in the butter using a fork until the mixture resembles breadcrumbs.

Using a fork, whisk together the milk and eggs in a jug. Whisk this liquid quickly into the flour mixture, then gently fold in the blueberries with a rubber spatula.

Fill the paper cases two-thirds full. Bake the muffins in the middle of the oven for 25 minutes until risen and golden brown. Leave in the tins for a few minutes, then remove and transfer to a wire rack. Serve warm, or as soon as possible after baking.

KEY TO PERFECTION

For light-as-air muffins, you must mix quickly and lightly. This is especially important when making fruit muffins as there's more mixing involved.

After whisking the liquid into the dry ingredients, gently fold the blueberries through the mixture using a spatula. Do this as quickly as possible, and don't try to make the mixture smooth – it should be sloppy and lumpy.

INDEX

ACKNOWLEDGMENTS

Marcus Wareing would like to thank…

I am indebted to many people who have helped me with this book, but in particular I would like to thank my wife, Jane, for her love and support, and my young sons, Jake and Archie, who seem to be expressing a desire for cooking – or the camera. I'm not sure which.

I would also like to thank my chefs – Alyn Williams for his help in getting the recipes together, and Darren Velvick for assisting me on the photo shoots. A personal thank you, too, to all the team at Pétrus, who run the restaurant so smoothly when I'm not there, especially Jean-Philippe at the front and Tristan in the kitchen. And thank you Gordon, Chris, and Holdings, for your support, and Jo and Nicky at Sauce Communications.

Special thanks are also due to Mary-Clare Jerram at Dorling Kindersley, for giving me the opportunity to express myself on the page; to photographer David Loftus for making the food look so good; Rosie Scott and Abbie Kornstein for assisting on the photo shoots; and to Alex, Emma, and Saskia at Smith & Gilmour, whose art direction, styling, and design have made the book stunning. I would also like to say how grateful I am to Angela Nilsen, who meticulously tested every recipe.

Last but by no means least, a massive thank you to my co-author, Jeni Wright, for her patience and skill in helping me write my first book. Her attention to detail and relentless quest for perfection have been amazing. She has driven me insane – but the end result is worth it.

Dorling Kindersley would like to thank…

Norma MacMillan for her outstanding editorial skill and professionalism, Ariane Durkin for her excellent editorial assistance, Caroline de Souza for her invaluable design assistance, and also to Hilary Bird for producing the index.

Cover photograph credits: Grooming by Honest Makeup using Mitch by Paul Mitchell. Styling by Boo Attwood using Label Lab white cotton shirt at House of Fraser www.houseoffraser.co.uk